THE MINDFUL GOLFER'S MANIFESTO

THE MINDFUL GOLFER'S MANIFESTO

SHOOTING PAR ON AND OFF THE COURSE

EDDIE OWSIAN

For Coaching Inquiries:

coacheddieocean@gmail.com

For Barbara Lynn and Artie Apple
whose love for a golf balls flight encouraged
a young man to soar, descend,
and soar again to greater heights

Table of Contents

A Quick Bucket at the Range

Enlightenment is a funny thing. Some say you must give up all worldly possessions and begin a meager life in solitude devoted to others and raising the vibration of a planet in peril through continued prayer. Expressing unconditional universal love to all of God's creatures.

I say it's the moment just before I hit a knockdown 6 iron. Relaxed. No thoughts. Full commitment to the shot. A divine sense of peace. It's such a beautiful day. And I'm here with my buddies. Nowhere on earth that I would rather be. A deep breath. I'm just about to pull the trigger and . . . wait . . . the wind is finally dying down? Have I become one with the universe and it is communicating with me? I throw up a few blades of grass to induce the Spirit of the Wind to be my guide. But now it blows even more in my face, and I realize I may need a 5 iron.

Where did that golf ball come from? Has the group behind me lost its patience? I take a look back. They most certainly have. I grab a 5-iron and address the ball. Where was I? Oh yes, choke down a little, play it back in my stance, aim a little right, keep my follow-through low, and my hands square. I got this. Another ball come whizzing by me . . . couldn't they at least yell "Fore"?! Maybe they want to hit me. Screw it. Just swing the damn club before you get a Pinnacle 2 in your ass. I take the club back, but something doesn't feel right. I do my best to correct my backswing in real time but end up bending my knees a bit and hitting 3 inches behind the ball. As I watch the remains of the shallow grave that I just dug fly through the air, my ball heads towards and then lands in the bunker 40 yards short of the green. Son of a bitch! I had that shot! I know that shot! I slam my club into my bag and prepare to give the finger to the foursome of assholes behind me. Incoming!! I gun my golf cart to evade another salvo and thankfully watch the bounding ball roll next to me as I haul ass out of the fairway.

As I said, enlightenment is a funny thing. Turns out, sometimes the joke is on me.

My handicap is a solid 5 currently. I never want it to go up or down anymore. It gives me an excuse to card a 72 or 87, no problem, without raising any eyebrows. Driving the ball well, hitting a bunch of greens, making some putts or OBs on Hole 3 and 11, skulling it out of the bunker, lipping out for a triple on 15 . . . I've been there. I've done it all. If you need me to be a scratch golfer to write this book, well . . . no such luck. I have no desire to consistently shoot par. I know the kind of work it takes and how stressful it is to maintain. Besides, I have a day job.

One thing has never changed throughout my life. That is, any day I plan to play golf immediately becomes awesome. I feel it in my stomach. The excitement. The nervousness. The visions. The day revolves around my teeing it up. Things cease to bother me and somehow, I am able to coast through my daily machinations. Maybe you are the same. I hope you look forward to playing a round a fraction as much as I do. It could be that it's a way to bond with my family or that I love watching the pros try to pull off the same shot as me. There is a connection, a relationship that consumes my attention. And much like any kid who says 3, 2, 1 and heaves a basketball shot to beat the buzzer, golf promises the chance to experience a sliver of glory. It's that kind of hope, which will bring you back to this awesome game over and over again.

This book aims to help the below-average golfer become above-average and stay there. I'll try to do that by showing you how to look at the game from a different perspective. After that, you are on your own. A local pro and an ample amount of perfect practice will get you in the A Flight consistently, going forward.

The secret I would like to impart is that golf mirrors our lives. We can use challenges on the golf course to become better people off the golf course. Conversely, personal self-development can lead to lower scores. It's simple really, and deep down you may already intuitively get this. Together we will explore some of the ways golf and life relate. Does this mean avoiding life's hazards will improve your chances of staying out of the drink? Possibly. You may naturally begin to avoid entering hazards. Sure, there will still be times when things happen that are out of your control. Your ball could catch a sprinkler head and bound into the trap just like you could get rear-ended while stopped at a traffic light. I'm not talking about those things. But the things that ARE in your control will change, like your attitude. Your body language. Your choices. Your breathing. Just to name a few. Easier said than done? That's up to you. We bring our current state of being into our golf game. Super competitive in life? Super competitive on the course. Relaxed with that downhill 10-footer for birdie on 18? Relaxed while popping the question to your girlfriend. Our state of consciousness transfers to our golf game and vice versa. My belief is that we can improve our golf game by elevating our conscious *awareness*.

We will start from the beginning and then go in-depth, using current physiological data, proven psychological theories, and (dare I say) spiritual concepts to permanently catapult your game on and off the course in the right direction. This is a no U-Turn process. You will not be able to unlearn what I teach you. There are fundamentals woven into these chapters that cannot be compromised. So, if your score and your experience on the course are dialed in just right, enjoy this book for entertainment purposes, have a laugh, and squeeze out a nugget or two of wisdom. But, if you are ready for a paradigm-shifting read with insights you can apply anytime, anywhere, especially on the golf course, then sit back with an open mind and follow me down the gopher hole. You might just be the next Cinderella story.

On the Practice Green

When people ask me how I got into golf, I tell them that back in the summer of 1983, I'd hit balls on my own range between shifts as a cook and a bartender. Usually, I get the response "Cool." and then, "Oh, wait, if you're 49 now, wouldn't 1983 make you an 11-year-old?" So, I tell them it would, but to be fair, I was 11½ and, you know, those half years were a big deal back then.

I was a bit of a punk growing up. Suspended from school here, in a fight there . . . always getting caught sneaking onto buses to go to the mall, nickel dime stuff. I never got into *hardcore* punk stuff, just enough to piss off the wrong person at the wrong time.

That person was my mother Barbara, and that time was during her divorce from my dad. With all the stresses of her own life and becoming a newly minted single mom, she had no time for my BS. And I was serving it up hot on a daily basis. My best friend Bobby lived 3 houses down in our suburban town of Mount Vernon, New York, only five short miles from

The Bronx, where the rest of my family had grown up. At that age, trouble just seemed to find us. Not that we minded.

One day, my mother sat me down to tell me she was at her wits end with my shenanigans. She was no angel herself growing up, and she'd given me plenty of free passes. But you give a kid an inch and he thinks he's a ruler. She'd "had it up to here" with me, and I knew it. But how bad could it be right? Grounded for a week; take my Atari away; household chores? I could take all that on the chin. This time though, her vibe was different. My younger sister, Mary, was there playing the role of bailiff and enjoying every minute of it no doubt. I was nothing short of a living nightmare to her life at the time. Mary read out my current local violations and crimes against humanity with as stern a stare as a 9-year-old can muster. Barbara, now presiding over this judgment, was very calm. Her fingers were entwined into clasped hands, much like she held them at St. Peter and Paul Catholic Church during prayer. I thought to myself, "This is not a good sign."

After a slight pause, Barbara read my sentence. She cleared her throat and said, "Your video games will not be taken from you this time, nor will you be grounded, as the court realizes these punishments are ineffective." I exhaled and finally started to relax. Cool. See, this is going to be just fine. Then another pause. Her Honor continued with a small smile and the slightest of squints, "You are hereby sentenced to 8 weekends of hard labor with your grandfather, Artie, in The Bronx at Van Cortlandt Golf Course. You will be dropped off on Friday after dinner and will return no sooner than Sunday evening when you will do your homework and go straight to bed. You will rise at 4:30 a.m. on Saturday and Sunday to do the bidding of said grandfather. Your only reprieve will be a single mid-afternoon nap. This sentence is final with no opportunity for an appeal. Your first parole hearing will commence at the end of your school year on June 14th. This court is adjourned." Or something like that.

"No!" I cried, "Not the weekend, not The Bronx, and definitely not Artie!!! Please, anything but that!! Don't make me go!!!" I threw myself on the kitchen floor in a half-assed tantrum and begged the court for mercy while the laughter of my friends rang in my mind amid visions of Wiffle Ball home runs and Ringalevio games. Judge Barbara scolded me by grabbing a wooden spoon and slamming it down on the counter. "This court is adjourned, Sir!!" My mother's Parliamentarian curly white hair parted in the middle and down to her shoulders did not help. The previous bailiff, who was now laughing in the adjacent dining room, was replaced by our family German Shepherd, Lola. She licked my ears like dogs do when you are a kid rolling on the floor, encouraging me to get up and pull myself together before I was found in contempt. I got up and ran to my room crying and hatching a plan to run away. Far, far away. Far from this God-forsaken place!

But then I realized something awful. I didn't own a red handkerchief to put all my kid's stuff in. Nor did I have a long stick to tie it to and throw over my shoulder! And where was I going to find a long piece of straw to put in my mouth? I live in the suburbs! I collapsed back onto the floor of my room, sobbing uncontrollably. Isn't that how everyone begins their golf career?

My grandfather Arthur Appel was of German descent. I knew this because he was great at math and always on time. I'm sure there are people who can appreciate these characteristics, but being an adolescent, I was not one of them. He was also a no-nonsense type of fella, along with being as sharp and witty as they come. He loved going to Manhattan College to hear lectures and stayed an avid reader until the day he died. But underlying his public appearance was a volcanic temper. Maybe being sent away to a farm in upstate New York after stealing an orange as a hungry kid or his unfortunate experience as a sailor in the greatest Naval disaster of all time, the shipwreck of the Truxton and the Pollux, had something to do with it. The book <u>Standing Into Danger</u> details the horrific account, which occurred in Newfoundland in the winter of 1942. PTSD was not diagnosed back in those days. Doctors just called it "shell shock" or whatever, and it wasn't considered treatable. Men usually medicated themselves with booze and my grandfather was no different. Thankfully, Artie survived his alcoholism and was instrumental in helping countless other men and women on their path back to sobriety during his 40 years in AA. And now he was my boss. Yay me!

While most kids were sound asleep dreaming of morning cartoons and their favorite sugary cereal, I was awakened by a 71-year-old man wearing translucent boxer shorts. He would swing open the door to my Aunt Lorraine's former room, flip on the light, and say, "Wake up, we're running late." The clock would always read somewhere around 4:11 a.m. and I would struggle to make sense of how he could reasonably combine "that time" and "running late." My grandmother had passed the year prior so the idea of seeing a loving face and a warm breakfast was no longer a possibility to be had. Nope, it was just me, my half-naked grandfather, and a bowl of cold Shredded Wheat. He'd scarf down his cereal while smoking a Parliament and reading the Daily News sports section. I would try not to make eye contact. That first morning, when he got up from the thin clear plastic-covered table, I realized his once see-through underwear were no longer on his body, and his undercarriage was fully exposed. I quickly looked away only to hear him boasting, "No need to be embarrassed. It's where you came from." Good talk, Grandpa. I sarcastically thought to myself, "These next 2 months are going to be awesome!" Then, I proceeded to walk over to the window of his 5th-floor, 83-degree apartment on 263rd St. to contemplate taking my own life.

The job I worked at Van Cortlandt Park while serving my sentence was, all in all, a good one. Highly illegal and begging for a visit from Social Services, but a good one, nonetheless. I didn't have the wherewithal at the time to understand, but looking back now, that place shaped me into the person I am today, and for that, I am very thankful.

Among the lessons were:

- How not to kill people with food
- How to hit the 40-yard pitch shot
- How to haggle by selling used golf balls
- How to hit the 15-yard flop shot
- How to mix a tangy kick-ass Bloody Mary
- How to chip and putt

My day would begin when it was still dark out, as you can imagine. I would wipe the morning dew off the first 20-ish golf carts, fill them up with gas, and line them up perfectly. Artie said all this practice would benefit me when I eventually got my driver's license, and he turned out to be right. I can still remember the look on the DMV tester's face when he instructed me to parallel park and I nailed it on the first try, one-handed. Then I would head to the kitchen, where I worked as a short-order cook for the early golfers affectionately known as "ham and eggers" and some locals who said they just liked the coffee and the scenery. To be fair, there was a nice lake. I won't get into the array of folks who tumble into a golf course diner at 5:30 a.m. in New York City. Let's just say I wound up fluent in broken English.

Eventually, I would mess up someone's order. They would complain, "The eggs weren't over-medium ENOUGH." What does that even mean?

Anyway, Artie would deal with these situations exactly as you would expect. He would go over to the customer, calmly inspect their $1.95 breakfast, gaze compassionately into the customer's eyes, and then quickly turn to me and yell at the top of his lungs, "YOU'RE FIRED!" Then, he would gently place the half-eaten breakfast down and inform the customer that the rest of their breakfast would magically taste delicious. The first time that happened I actually got a little excited thinking I was free from my line cooking punishment. Then the dishwashing ginzo out on parole snapped, "Don't get too moist, kid. I got fired 4 times last Sunday." So much for that.

Around 9am, I would try to fire up the diesel golf cart with the trailer hitch. This beast of burden was infamous for breaking down and somehow our Polish maintenance guy Ludwik seemed to think the only thing missing from the motor was loud foreign profanity. He would lift the seat, stare into the chassis, shake his head, and deliver a stern X-rated rant. A twist here, a tinker there, then another scolding. After a while, Artie would kick open the back door to the kitchen and yell, "Hey, Warsaw, while we're young!" Usually, Ludwik would threaten Artie with whatever wrench happened to be in his hand, and sometimes, well, depending on his blood sugar levels, he would just throw it.

Eventually, the cart would start, and the enclosed trailer that was my second 8' x 4' workspace of the day would get hitched onto the back of it, collapsing whatever was left of the poor suspension. Somehow Ludwik thought pumping the tires up with more air would help. Spoiler Alert: It never did.

Then there was the Head Pro, Colin. To be honest, I didn't see much of him, but I really wanted his job. The position duties essentially added up to hiding behind a newspaper reclined in your chair while placing your worn-out Footjoys on the corner of the desk. He was one of my first idols. A man who'd made it to the pinnacle of the golf world, although he had a reputation for being a bit of a drinker and a lover of gambling on the ponies. One time when I asked him if he thought my grip was too strong or too weak, he just replied, "We got a problem in the 5th today." I figured it meant I should go with what I got. Less is more, right? I was unaware that the "company" who managed the golf course on paper had hired him directly from Scotland as a sort of prop.

No one else liked Colin because, at the first sign of rain, he would flip down the corner of the New York Post, gaze outside, and yell, "Shut her down, boys!" Then, he'd high tail it out of there and head to the horse racetrack, no doubt. Still, I dreamed of eventually having his job and being hated like that. At my age, I just thought everyone was jealous he could leave the place anytime he wanted and go on the PGA Tour. He was a pro! What's the problem? PGA Tour Pros are . . . pros . . . and this guy is a pro, too! He's just CHOOSING to be here. For us. The little people. He could probably make a hole-in-one whenever he wanted! God, I wanted to be him so bad. Come to think of it, I could do without the puffy pink nose and all the slurring though. Ahhh, a boy and his dreams.

I would park in the median hardpan of 3 well-worn cart paths when I arrived at my final designated spot out at the crossroads of the 2nd, 8th, and 14th holes. My superiors would give me one of those long lighters to ignite the propane boilers for the hotdogs and sauerkraut because, yeah, that's what you gave an 11-year-old kid back in the early '80s. I would rely on my comprehensive training to keep me safe, which amounted to, "If it smells too much like gas when you are lighting the pilot, just wave your hand back and forth for a few seconds before trying again." Not exactly OSHA complaint, but adults were taller than me, so I just assumed they knew everything.

Ten minutes later, everything would be heating up

just right. The packaged danishes were masterfully merchandised next to the cigarettes. My internal Doppler told me when it was going to be a hot one. I'd think, "These golfers are going to love me; I just know it. Everything chilled for them. I'm probably going to be the best lunch guy this course has ever had." I went through my inventory of drinks and threw them in the coolers picturing foursome after foursome cracking those babies open and toasting to me. "Here's to little Eddie!" they would exclaim, as they raised their drinks. Then they would throw dollar after dollar into the Maxwell House tin that Artie labeled "Orthodontics Fund" with masking tape, whatever that meant. Maybe even a 5 spot. Can you imagine?! OJ, RC Cola, Pepsi, Tab. Fresca, Sunkist, Mr. Pibb, Fanta. Budweiser, Schlitz, Coors, Schaefer. And a bunch of tiny little bottles with all kinds of weird names. I tried a little bit once because the baby bottles looked so cute, but it burned. Colin said laughingly that the golfers would help me figure those out later.

There was A LOT of downtime. I did enjoy sitting in a half-broken beach chair and listening to afternoon Yankee games on my transistor radio to help pass some of the afternoons away. I'll never forget hearing the announcer explain how George

Brett went psycho on the umpire during the infamous "Pine Tar Game." That whole situation was tough to grasp as a kid with no visuals.

Thankfully the golf cart I drove was parked facing the longest Par 5 in the country at that time. The 619-yard #2 hole. The fairway was so wide I would practice short pitch shots to the right of the tee box with a wedge Artie gave me from the lost and found bag along with two handfuls of old range balls. When I would finish ten shots, I would time how long it took me to run and pick them all up. I figured that the shorter the time was, the more consistent I must be striking since consistent shots would land the balls closer together. This is the shit you come up with as a kid with lots of time on your hands. And since I came up with that, I assumed NASA would be calling soon asking for more of my deductions.

Once I got bored with my running and gathering game, I would find a rare tuft of grass next to my cart and try to hit balls to the top of the tall pine tree just off the 2nd green. Then the balls would just be dispensed back down to the trunk Plinko-style. "Boy am I a genius or what," I thought. Every now and then I would get in the zone and hit ball after ball perfectly. Open stance, open face, keeping my head down, and releasing my wrist just right. The problem was that I would ignore the threesomes walking off the green who had to cover their heads, no doubt wondering where the fuck the golf ball making that unmistakable sound in the tree was coming from. One of them would always toss some colorful language in my direction in whatever dialect they happened to speak. I assumed they were pissed because they had lipped out for bogey.

On occasion, if there was a lapse in play, I would scoot over to the 2nd green. Emptying the bag of the world's worst golf balls, I'd choke down on the steel of the shaft and try to chip close to the hole. Then, I'd raise the wedge off the ground and try to putt it by sculling it toward the cup. If I got up and down, I would treat myself to a Root Beer "on the house." Ahhh, the spoils of victory!

One time the assistant greenskeeper, Flynn, saw me stroking a ball on the putting surface with a wedge. He proceeded to tell me that if he ever caught me doing it again, he'd do something with my balls that I wouldn't like very much. What did I care? The balls were beaten up so badly already. Artie informed me later those weren't the balls he was talking about. Going forward, I always remembered to snag a wedge AND a putter out of the lost and found bag behind Colin's desk.

There were a lot of characters out there and I was given strict orders by Artie to not take any BS from anyone. If there were any issues, I was instructed to use my walkie-talkie then and only then, to get the patrolling security officer, Rueben, out there pronto. But Rueben was the biggest shyster of them all. He would hold open the fence between holes 4 and 12 and let interlopers onto the course to play 9 holes. Then he'd let them back out through the fence. I knew this because he would slip me hush money. He said it was his "International Relations Program." Little did I know, it was more of a gambling racket for which he was the treasurer. I think some guys actually came from Jersey to play in those matches. One time, Reuben slipped me a Victoria's Secrets Catalog to keep me "occupado." I knew something was going down BIG TIME that day. High Stakes Underground Golf Tournaments? If you don't know, now you know.

Eventually, the day would wind down. During this, I learned a lot of things other pre-teens probably didn't, such as the following:

- what "on the rocks" means
- that mustard and sauerkraut ALWAYS go on a hot dog in New York (asking will just induce an uncomfortable look from your customer)

- found golf balls go for fifty cents each, sixty if it's a Titleist Balata
- golfers 3 down in their match will tip according to how much you are willing to "lean on" a Gin and Tonic they are whipping up for their opponent
- it's best to know "un poquito español"
- diesel gas stinks when you get it all over yourself
- how to drive in reverse with a trailer
- the best standards and practices for establishing "your cut of the action"
- refuse the offer of a cigarette from anyone from Eastern Bloc countries

Andre, the hungover second-shift worker at Van Cortlandt, would show up to replace me around two in the afternoon and I would grab my future dentist's money and take his cart back to the clubhouse. This was one of my favorite parts of the day. Why? Because he was usually late. He would remove the governor of the cart's gas line and that baby would fly. Sometimes after a little rain, I would crank up "Everybody's Working' for the Weekend" by Loverboy on my Walkman, floor the gas pedal, cut the wheel to the left, lock up the brakes and spin my ass down the slight hill that was fairway #2. With all the trees on the course, no one saw me. Happiness is.

Artie and I would head back toward his apartment building in the Bronx, stop at the deli, and get in a little snooze. Then back to the golf course we went, to get in a free-of-charge late afternoon 9 holes. Artie taught me about strong grips, flat swings, and flier lies; when to bump and run, when to spin it; how to hit a bunker shot, and how to hit a knockdown. He had names for all his shots, too. Snappy, Slappy, Cutty, Loopy, Bumpy, Scooty, Punchy, Spanky. You get the picture. He would talk to his swing and address the ball as if it was a third party. "C'mon, Spanky, get your ass out there and give me a short iron in!" "Here we go Loopy, stop on a dime!" "Alright, Bumpy. You haven't been worth a shit all season, but I know you got it in you!" You know. Normal stuff. Artie basically had an outer "inner monologue" and when he approved of his result, the look on his face said there was nowhere in the universe he'd rather be.

When we finished with 9, he would put the flag back in the cup, reach out his arm to shake my little 11-year-old hand, and say, "Thank you" because that's what you do. To me, his hands felt like baseball mitts you'd left out all winter. In a word, they were weathered. But do you know something? They were the hands of a man who'd held his own newborn. Those of a city kid who had to farm the earth in upstate NY. They were the hands that taught me how to cook so other people could eat. Hands that threw rock candy at honking cars from five stories up. Hands that held a baseball bat in the Semi-pro NYC baseball league. Hands he used to fight for his freedom, which clung to a frigid cliff while he watched his buddies permanently snatched back into the cold, dark, unforgiving sea. He'd placed those hands on the shoulders of friends in the throes of seemingly hopeless addiction. Artie had repentant hands that merged and pointed upward to the heavens on Sundays.

And for a moment, I held one of those hands. And felt like his equal.

A Little History Lesson

"Golf is an exercise which is much used by a gentleman in Scotland . . . a man would live 10 years longer for using this exercise once or twice a week."
- Dr. Benjamin Rush (1745 – 1813)

"I shall use the exercise of golf three or four times a week in order to live 20 years longer.
For the sake of my family, of course."
- A man

Imagine with me that many, many, years ago, your homeland, the place you and your lineage have called home for generations, was set to be invaded by a formidable enemy. We will call this interloping threat to your land, women, and children, the Assholes Undermining Lad's Desires or the "A.U.L.D." for short. You and your buddies were commanded by The Grand High Exalted Mystic Ruler to prepare for battle by training and perfecting military tactics such as catapulting, archery, and the preparation of boiling oil. The freedom of your glorious realm was in your hands and the awaiting menace was slowly closing in. The only caveat was that you and 11 of your closest companions had an 11:37, 11:47, and 11:57 tee time at the local golf links. As an honorable gentleman, you would no doubt uphold your just and worthy cause by announcing, "Only under the penalty of law shall we the people, **cancel** a recorded tee time! We are righteous men who hold our word to be true! We are also 20 pence in arrears to our competition and have grand designs on becoming all square!" Then, as fate would have it, The Royal Family might declare, "The sport of golf is hereby banned entirely for no less than 45 years under the penalty of incarceration!"

In fact, the time was 1457, the King was James II, and the place was on the east coast of Scotland. Cooler heads thankfully prevailed and the ban was largely ignored, which paved the way for the sport you and I love so much. The rest, shall we say, is history.

The sport of golf could not have had more humble beginnings. It literally started with some dude's simple fascination with seeing how a pebble, when struck with a crooked stick, would clear a Scottish sand dune. Now why would that activity spark the future worldwide phenomenon known as golf? I speculate that there may have been a wager or two involved.

I can just see it, the world's first golfer announcing, "Two pence for a tally of five in a row over Ye Old Sand Dune henceforth known as Jamieson's Corner!"

"Precisely!" replies the gallery.

Ironically enough, during his initial swing, our world's first golfer became distracted by the collapse and subsequent face-plant of the shire's local drunkard, Alister Mulligan. It was determined by the assembly of men that our "original forefather" would be granted another swipe at said pebble in the interest of all that is fair and just. I am speculating here. I do not want to go on the official record as the one who said this is how "The Mulligan" was originally determined. But if *you* said it in a public forum, I wouldn't put too much effort into having it stricken.

In 1502, the inaugural Seal of Approval was issued by the Honorable King James IV who was also a solid 6 handicap. He was proud to be the world's first golfing monarch and is said to have possessed a soft draw so refined as to have matched the "curvature of a baby's bottom." This royal endorsement allowed our glorious game to spread across Europe during the 16th century, led by Mary Queen of Scots and her husband King Charles.

While studying in France, Queen Mary was accompanied by military cadets or "caddies" who were well-known for their ability to preserve Her Majesty's safety along with selecting the perfect club for a certain tricky downhill par 3. The finest golf course of the day was near Edinburgh at "Leith Municipal," which hosted the first iteration of the now popular Ryder Cup in 1682. The Duke of York and George Patterson representing Scotland, smoked two English noblemen 4 and 3. To make matters worse for the British contingency, Mr. Patterson mocked his opponents mercilessly after a tall glass of ale in the clubhouse, by using the Englishman's teeth to describe the direction of the foreigner's ball striking. And so, the international rivalries began.

The Gentlemen Golfers of Leith formed the first club in 1744 and the game of golf officially became a sport. They set up annual competitions in multiple locations using prizes that would no doubt appease the spouses of the newly minted golf pros – silver plates. I have every confidence that the wives back in the shire were THRILLED at the thought of their husbands traveling the countryside playing golf for a shiny silver plate to be displayed on the mantle while they single-handedly took care of the farm, livestock, and 13 children.

The first reference to golf and its historic hometown of St. Andrews was in 1552, but it was not until 1754 that the St. Andrews Society of Golfers was formed to compete in its own annual tournament using Gentlemen Golfers of Leith's rules. Duncan Forbes was the appointed commissioner and is responsible for devising the earliest draft of today's rulebook with entries not unlike the following: ". . . if your ball comes among water or any watery filth, you are at liberty to take out your ball and bring it behind the hazard and teeing it, you may play it with any club and allow your adversary a stroke to get out your ball."

Not much has changed in the last 250 years, has it?

At the time golfers generally used hand-crafted wooden clubs made from beech, with shafts of ash or hazel. Golf balls back then were assembled using compressed feathers wrapped in a stitched horse hide. I can only hypothesize that this is why the first "low score that wins a hole" was called a skin. On the course and in the clubhouse, conversations of the day surely included trying various golf clubs and playing at different courses throughout Scotland and England. There must have been a very strong buzz about these desires amongst the golfers of these mighty kingdoms because the Industrial Revolution emerged soon thereafter. Now I am NOT saying that the sport of golf initiated the Industrial Revolution because that would be highly irrational and speculative, but I AM saying that I am pretty sure that we should be thanking golf for bringing about the *worldwide* Industrial Revolution. I know everyone has been wondering for all these years about the catalyst that took our planet from a place in the galaxy where things were only made by hand, to one that incorporates machinery into manufacturing. Now, once again I'm just spitballin' here, but it MUST have been golf. It all just adds up. Clearly, it explains the advent of cars and later on the shortage of horses, on account of all the golf balls needed to be made. That part is an indisputable fact. Maybe.

Across the pond in the newly formed United States of America, erections OF golf courses and FOR golf courses were happening on a massive scale. Not only did this naturally lead to a baby boom, but also to the establishment of no less than 900 golf courses by the turn of the century. Legend has it that in 1888, two Scotsman from Dunfermline, John Reid and Robert Lockhart, demonstrated golf by setting up a sneaky long dogleg left Par 4 in an apple orchard in Yonkers, New York that always played into the wind. Reid, America's first Head Pro, established "Saint Andrew's Golf Club" later that same year due to the backlog in tee times and notorious slow play.

Eventually, mayhem ensued countrywide, and our game needed a governing body, due to a wide variance in local grounds rules, arguments over restrictions on pin placements, and just straight-up cheating. In 1894, the "Golf Association of these here United States of America" formed and shortly thereafter condensed itself to just the U.S.G.A. Through a tremendous influx of commercial funding and sponsorships, the U.S.A. became the center for professional golf. Then a Dutch foursome of gentlemen emerged seemingly out of the woodwork, insisting that their ancestors had been playing a game called "kolf" in the settlement of Fort Orange near Albany, New York since 1650 and boldly claimed responsibility for the game's inception. They were reminded by the U.S.G.A. that it was in fact the Scottish who brought the game here and that it was played during the spring, summer, and fall months in local fields not unlike their beloved home country.

The men from Holland laughed at this and stated emphatically that their robust grandfathers played "kolf" during the winter as well, using the same rules. The first "golf clap" ensued thereafter, deferring the birth of our game in America to the gentlemen from Holland.

I pieced together the history of golf through painstaking hours of research and cross-referencing. Interviews were also conducted to bring you the bona fide truth, so help me Google. I will admit, I put a little mustard on some of those facts, but the overarching story is legit, and the point is that golf is here and it's here to stay. Some conspiracy theorists even suggest that golf was invented by Scottish Freemasons, that it constituted the original "secret society" and was to be played only by the local governing men of influence. They point to the Grand Master Secretary Mason of Scotland, Alexander McDougall, as being the captain of both Leith golfers known as the "Honorable Company" and the "Royal and Ancient" St. Andrews golfers. No doubt he was elected to the post of the Grand Master Secretary of the Scottish Rite, what with his innate ability to juggle all those foursomes, handicap the hackers, and divvy up the prize pool for "Ye Ole Skins Game." Regardless of how it started, I am glad it did so that we can enjoy ourselves for four or five hours every now and then. With any luck, it will continue to inspire the generations to come with visions of greenies, sandies, and birdies.

Hole 1, Par 5: BREATH

"One way to break up any tension
is good deep breathing."
- Byron Nelson

Your life depends on breathing, and this is never more apparent than when applied to the game of golf. The single most important insight within these pages and the basis for all other learning herein is the following: YOU MUST RELEARN HOW TO CONSCIOUSLY BREATHE. Try to stop breathing for a couple of minutes and you will find, without needing much convincing from me, that breathing is our most fundamental physical activity. Drawing in atmospheric energy and releasing elements back into the air can differentiate a day with vitality or lethargy. Volumes have been written in dedication to the breath and how it governs our lives. The New York Times Bestseller "Breathe" by James Nestor is one such offering. He explores the past, present, and future of our inhaling and exhaling human species, and rightfully claims that "Respiration is, at its core, reciprocation." In making the case for nasal breathing, Nestor explains that it controls our temperature, blood pressure, and mood. Correct breathing induces an engagement with our environment and connects parts of ourselves with our surroundings.

And yet, growing up here in the ole US of A, I never learned how to breathe properly. Did you? The message I received was more like, "*Breathing? What of it? You just did it, didn't you? If you haven't passed out – congratulations!*" Could we set our standards any lower? Think about it. Here we have BREATH, a life force, as abundant as the cosmos, so powerful as to enable the trillions of little miracles occurring in our bodies on a moment-by-moment basis, and we just kind of wing it.

In the article "Every Breath You Take," Julia Mercado tells us that deep breathing stimulates the vagus nerve, which is responsible for connecting our brain and gut. Activating this nerve relaxes our bodies and eases us out of fight or flight mode. While shallow breathing communicates to our primal selves that we are preparing to run from a threat, deep breathing reassures us that, for the moment, we are

OK.

Golfspeak translation: Deep breathing intensifies our "gut feeling," the one that tells us when a shot is playing longer than it looks and urges us to take out that extra club. If you can learn to listen to and trust your gut feelings, you will gain the confidence to make those necessary split-second decisions on the course. This inner knowing is shrouded by unconsciousness, low levels of stress in the body.

Study after study has connected diaphragmatic breathing to lower levels of cortisol in the blood and less oxidative stress on the body. In 2017, a very extensive study was conducted by Beijing University titled "The Effect of Diaphragmatic Breathing on Attention, Negative Affect, and Stress in Healthy Adults." It explored the effects of breathing into the belly (diaphragmatic breathing) relative to "normal" breathing into the chest. Cortisol, a steroid hormone released in response to stress, has been associated with depression, anxiety, and other negative emotions. Anxiety is the sworn enemy of the golfer. Anxiety will cause you to doubt yourself, doubt your swing, and doubt your ability. The nervous system, blood pressure, and heart rate all go haywire in the presence of anxiety. PGA Member Marc Soloman of Golf Made Simple implores that, unequivocally, skill level goes down when anxiety levels go up. The good news is that this means if anxiety levels drop, skill levels will automatically rise.

Let's look deeper at how to release this bogey-making emotion. The first step is to simply bring awareness to your anxiety by creating an observer within your own mind whose only job is to watch the uncomfortable feeling. Next, breathe through your nose down deep into your belly. Gradually, you will feel a shift in your consciousness accompanied by an increased sense of ease and well-being. You will find that a natural rhythm, pace, and flow to your breath has emerged to bring you more focused clarity.

It wasn't until Eastern philosophers traveled west roughly 150 years ago, that breath began to receive attention from the collective consciousness. Yoga, Tai Chi, Qi Gong, meditation, and the like, were founded on the movement of breath since oxygenating the body is paramount to overall health. Without adequate oxygen, the body, metaphorically, must swim upstream to maintain equilibrium.

Have you ever watched a sleeping infant breathe? They're great at it! They breathe in through their nose and all the way into their cute, delicate little bellies. They do this naturally. Babies understand instinctively that respiration must be optimized to survive and thrive at such a crucial age of development. This display confirms to me that we are designed to bring oxygen into the recesses of our diaphragm. We are designed to allow the nasal cavity to filter and warm the air so our bodies can absorb all the elements we need. Our current way of receiving and releasing air needs to be revamped in order to maximize our full potential as human beings.

Unlearning detrimental habits is just as important as employing beneficial routines because space must open in our consciousness to allow new patterns to develop. One thing's for sure, if breathing can sustain life, we'd better learn to master it on and off the golf course.

Everything in this book builds on the fundamental skill of correct breathing. Focus on your awareness and trust that a relaxed, comfortable state of mind and body breeds consistency. So, how do we integrate these principles into our game? For starters, we must recognize that the golf swing itself is identical to the in-and-out breath cycle. Imagine the in-breath as the backswing, and the out-breath as the downswing. Simple, right?

Whether breathing or swinging, we must complete both stages in full, otherwise, we're going to have issues. Our swing tempo must mimic a relaxed, even-keeled, unforced inflow and outflow of air. *A well-controlled, smooth backswing builds energy and confidence. A strong but unrushed downswing with a full follow-through releases power.* The golfing gods will ultimately determine where the ball ends up, but we can feel sure we've done our part if we show up with a smooth and steady swing. Dead solid perfect contact with the ball is the feeling that keeps us coming back to this crazy game. That feeling says, "I can do this!"

Over time, controlled and relaxed breathing will positively impact our scorecard. One interesting swing tactic suggested by Ph.D. Gay Hendricks in his book *Conscious Golf,* is to wait to swing until you are fully relaxed after a small but full exhale. This, he argues, will release any pent-up tension, resistance, or constriction.

A pre-shot routine that I highly recommend:
Stand behind the ball and visualize a perfect shot along with the feeling of HAVING ALREADY EXECUTED that shot to the best of your ability. Use as much imagination as you need. Then address the ball while breathing comfortably through the nose. Take one last look at the target, then a deep, relaxed, belly breath in through the nose and then out (via the nose or mouth) releasing any tension on the exhale,

and let 'er rip. After a full complete follow-through, enjoy a nice, deep, inhale again and revel in your handiwork. (Or yell "FORE!" because you know, this is golf after all, and we don't want anyone getting killed out there.)

Another technique: Inhale on the backswing and exhale on the downswing.

Emma Ferris, breathing coach and physiotherapist describes it best: "I'd like to tell you that it's as simple as breathing in on your backswing and breathing out as you follow through, but there are a few more factors that influence how you breathe with golf. The reality is that inhaling on your backswing and exhaling on your follow-through will allow for increased mobility and will help with force transfer from your lower body and through the club. With golf, your core muscles need to be strong enough to transfer force generated from the legs and the torque of the golf swing through the upper limb."

Try out these techniques on the range. First, hit some balls and notice your normal current breathing rhythm without judgment. Just observe. It may be perfect for you. You can always come back to it. Then try the two breathing modalities mentioned above. Breathing in and out before starting your swing, **and** breathing in on the backswing, out on the downswing. Don't worry about where the ball goes. Focus on finding the "feel" and bringing greater mindfulness to your game. Mindfulness, and the sensations of relaxation, focus, and calm awareness, are key for taking any aspect of your life to the next level. It feels profound once you've grasped it, so don't blame me if you end up in a Buddhist monastery. Just watch out for the Lama. Big hitter.

Hole 2, Par 4: ATTITUDE

"A bad attitude is worse than a bad swing."
- Payne Stewart

Our attitude defines our round. Let me say that again: Our attitude defines our round.

This was famously depicted for us on the classic sitcom, *The Honeymooners*. This legendary 1955 TV show was known for its over-the-top antics and charismatic character lineup. One such character included the beloved Ed Norton, the best sewer worker in Bensonhurst, Brooklyn. In one memorable scene, Ed reads a book on the golf swing to the star of the show and lovable loser, Ralph Kramden. Sitting in the kitchen of Ralph's apartment one morning, Norton instructs Ralph on the first and foremost step in producing the correct golf swing, "Address the ball."

Then, Norton interprets the direction all too literally. "Step up. Plant your feet firmly . . . HELLO,

BALL!"

Immediate. Legend. Status.

Other than a good laugh, what is there to learn from this gesture? A lot, actually. We play golf to enjoy ourselves. Never forget that. Enjoyment becomes near impossible when we're over-identifying with our game and our score. Taking the game, and ourselves, too seriously can become debilitating to the extent that it screws up our round of golf in the worst possible way. I mean, it's not like we're not on the PGA Tour. Unless you are, in which case this principle of enjoyment still applies.

We are physically capable of swinging a club. We get to savor the outdoors. We have the time to laugh with our buddies. We are blessed with good exercise and with the opportunity to learn new things. To celebrate a good shot. The game of golf lets us encourage others, display honorable etiquette, and leave our daily troubles on the practice green. Golf is a rare gift that keeps on giving, one which deserves our positive attitude and appreciation.

The secret to a premier round of golf is counter intuitive. That is, **we MUST release any expectations of the outcome.** I know it sounds strange but hear me out. Our job as golfers is to consider all the pre-shot factors (distance, wind, etc.)

and then put the best swing on the ball we can. *That's pretty much it.* Beyond fine-tuning our attention to those details, the results should be considered out of our hands.

Consider this scenario: You mishit a ton of shots but get every break known to man and wind up shooting a much lower score than usual. How would you feel? Probably not too good, knowing as sure as hell it won't happen the next time you play. Your greatest reward may be winning a few bucks off your chums. Conversely, imagine a scenario in which you strike the ball beautifully every time but can't catch a break, and wind up shooting above your handicap. You'd still feel awful.

Do you see what I'm getting at? The breaks you get out on the course ultimately have nothing to do with you. The only thing that matters in the end is how you conduct yourself.

The spirit of golf deserves your best conduct.

Russian physicist Vadim Zeland details the concept of "excess potential" in his book, *Reality Transurfing Steps I-V.* I would encourage anyone interested in taking their life and game to the next level to read his works. "Excess potential," Zeland says, is created by placing too much importance (and all the over-emotion that accompanies it) on a desired outcome. For perspective's sake, imagine for a moment the feelings that might overtake a person fleeing from a burning house. Those are the feelings of importance to the max. Your importance levels in that scenario would be way higher than they would upon casually exiting a house that isn't up in flames.

Playing quality golf requires us to lower importance on where the ball ends up, and instead simply focus on making a smooth, relaxed swing. To bring it back around to the game of golf, let's say you have a shot from 150 yards out, and feel that you *should* be able to hit a 7 iron to about 3 feet. Is it possible? Yes. But is it realistic? Instead, you end up short and to the left of the green, on the fringe, but below the hole. Under normal circumstances, it is a relatively easy up and down. Heck, you might even hole it out. But you are *so* upset with yourself or the world or God or whatever that you didn't knock it stiff, that your emotions get the best of you. You've been had by over-importance. Now, you're walking toward your ball ruminating on all the less-than-perfect decisions you've made that got you into this position instead of visualizing and sensing the feeling of your next shot going in, or at worst, a tap in for par.

Zeland suggests that "The Law of Balancing Forces" would step in at this point to even the playing field because nature is always seeking balance in every possible way. No matter if it's a solar system or an emotion, everything is energy, and that energy seeks balance. Sir Isaac Newton proved this with his Third Law.

Back to the next shot on the fringe. If you have yet to *let go* of the emotions associated with not knocking it stiff, your chances of chili-dipping or sculling your chip have increased (whether you like it or not) on account of the excess energy you've introduced to your game. If you can't promptly reestablish equilibrium (*by letting go*) botching the next two or three shots may be in your overall best interest if it means you'll once and for all release your grip on a perfect outcome. Whatever it takes. The cosmos encourages us to just LET GO. Immediately when we do, we begin moving steadily toward balance. You are familiar with the saying, "When it rains, it pours," aren't you? Consider that the tagline for "The Law of Balancing Forces." Eventually, we must release our heightened expectations and the heightened emotions they elicit. Because it can, and will, always pour harder. Don't believe me? YouTube - Jean Van De Velde at The Open Championship.

On a personal note, I share with you an expensive story from my own life to illustrate this law. With a sound mind and body, I made the decision to invest 5K in a cryptocurrency startup I believed was going to solve a real-world problem. The company was creating an app that would allow our planet's 1.3 billion adults without a bank account, to access financial services via cellphone. To me, the vision seemed innovative. I was patient for years as this company grew; I remained patient even as my portfolio began to lose its bulk.

Then, fast forward to the perfect storm: I had a bad week at work, the boss was on my case, customers were complaining more than usual, and everything kept breaking. Nothing was going my way. I let myself become so emotional that I hit a breaking point. All the patience I'd maintained in my investment ventures up to that point, just evaporated. I liquidated the remainder of my funds and decided to start a new career day trading with Bitcoin. *Spoiler Alert.* I lost all my funds. Six months later, the market surged. The company took off and I had officially lost out on 675K in potential profit.

I've since asked the online trading exchange if they'll let me take a mulligan. I'll keep you posted. Had I stayed emotionally balanced, I might be spending my days touring private golf clubs on beautiful islands, knocking back rum punches. If I had dropped *the importance* of a perfect week at work, I might be on the golf course right now instead of writing this book.

Back once more to the 150-yard shot.

You hit it well, but the wind knocks it down and lands your ball in the front right bunker. Do you have a better chance of getting up and down by letting go of the result as fast as possible or by stewing over Mother Nature's imposition? We both know the answer. In golf, as in life, it's wise to visualize and feel your desired result. But it is wiser still, to never let yourself become so emotionally attached to a perfect outcome that anything less throws you off your game. Golf generates cumulative emotions, one swing at a time. Master those feelings by rebelling against the status quo and *adopting a relentlessly positive outlook.*

Hole 3, Par 3: RELATIONSHIP

"The businessman – the man to whom age brings
golf instead of wisdom."
- George Bernard Shaw

During my sophomore year of college, I managed to find a job working in the bag room at Boca Grove Country Club in Boca Raton, Florida. This town is known all over Florida for being a golfer's paradise; golf course after golf course pepper the city, offering any golf lover a plethora of choices to "spoil a good walk" as Churchill once said. Some venues are open to the public, others are extremely exclusive. Punk from the suburbs that I was, who'd cut his teeth at a working man's course in the Bronx, there was only one kind of place I was seeking employment: at a super high-end swanky, country club! That's right! I'd paid my dues at a beat-up municipal course, and now it was high time I found out how the other half lived. I didn't care if I had to clean the groove of each member's club with a steel brush and polish their shoes with a fine chamois. It meant that in return, I'd get the privilege of playing on a multi-million-dollar track for free! I had a 2.14 GPA but, in my mind, acquiring this job was nothing short of genius.

While at Boca Grove, I was befriended by a man named Hartley Lord. Hartley was a man who'd earned and then spent an eight-figure fortune, not once, but four separate times. He loved the pressure of having to perform and thrive while solving problems that were monetizable. Most guys down there were retired but Hartley preferred to work. He said it kept his mind sharp.

One day I asked him when he'd first taken up the game, we both loved so much. "Not until I was well into my fifties," Mr. Lord told me. Knowing he was a financier and a good one at that, I asked, "Why so late?" Hartley said something I'll never forget. He said, "Because I eventually learned you can do more business in four hours playing golf on a Saturday than you can in a week of meetings."

I imagined him gambling up a storm and then realizing, being the novice he was back then, that he wasn't good enough to wager for high stakes. Mr. Lord explained that while his meetings tended to involve negotiations and intricate details, all his initial partnerships, pitches, ideas, strategies, intel, and so forth, got smoothly communicated over a round of golf. Light-hearted banter, the perfectly manicured fairways, powder-soft sand traps, a cocktail or two, and the occasional birdie, all coalesced to create a fertile ground for entrepreneurial endeavors.

In contrast to the competitive feeling of the office, a round of golf imposes less pressure to impress your partner, to manipulate or to maneuver conversation in a direction reeking of self-service. Instead, it's chatting while waiting for the group in front of you to putt out and meander off the green. It's just a game. Golf is best enjoyed in a state of relaxation.

You never know what'll happen. New ideas mentioned in passing while on the links may bounce around an investor's skull for a few holes until a light bulb goes off, spawning the infamous "have your people call my people." Businessmen love the excitement of new ventures; putting people to work, disrupting an industry, competing globally, and creating innovation, all stoke the fires of a capitalist mind. On a biological level, exciting new ventures release dopamine and its "get-up-and-go" cousin, adrenaline, which inspires and creates focus. The seasoned investor has a hard time ignoring money-generating ideas with merit and serious potential.

Would it surprise you to learn that million-dollar deals are frequently made on the golf course? It shouldn't. One of the most perfect settings to forge a potential partnership is during a round. Watching someone play, we get answers to questions we may not have even known we had: What is your partner's overall demeanor? How do they deal with challenges? How's their self-talk? Are they respectful of the rules? Are they competitive? Can they pivot strategies? How easily do they get rattled? Do they value follow-through? Can they keep their head down and focus?

The list goes on and on because *golf exposes everyone, for better or worse*. For four to five hours, the golfer demonstrates what they're made of. Body language and tone of voice reveal multitudes when we know what to look for. Potential clients or investors go with their gut most of the time, which means whatever information we're subconsciously communicating through non-verbal cues has the power to either break or seal a deal.

The 18-hole roller coaster ride via "the good walk, spoiled" tells our tale. The final scorecard means nothing. It's our display of conduct that's being tallied. Can we quickly let go of the dreaded "snowman" and get back on track? That's one positive trait a businessman will promptly translate into revenue-earning potential. And rightfully so.

Building strong rapport is the intention behind bringing the game of golf into the world of business. Rapport should be your goal during a round of golf with potential clients or investors, not lowering your handicap. Trust and understanding between two people lead to mutually beneficial circumstances. Prioritize rapport-building with the next new person you meet, and you will be surprised by the opportunities that open. One thing will lead to another, you'll see. And keep golf in mind as a game that offers up a tailor-made setting. No pun intended. Well, kind of.

Hole 4, Par 4: INTEGRITY

"The longer you play, the more certain you are
that a man's performance is the outward
manifestation of who, in his heart,
he really thinks he is."
- Hale Irwin

Do you trust yourself to "do the right thing" when no one is looking? The game of golf is eager to answer that question for us all and many other fundamental questions regarding our integrity. A wonderful thing reveals itself to us during a round of golf. That is *the essence of our character*. Character building is ongoing–the process by which we are defined. We all know how easy it is to improve a lie; to move our ball just a little when it's deep in a bunker, and mark six when it really was a seven. These internal dilemmas surface dozens of times throughout the round, giving us opportunity upon opportunity to evaluate and adjust our actions, choose integrity, and create a real WIN.

Life is all about stacking W's, those little moments throughout the day when we show ourselves, and the world at large, what we're made of. Wake up early. *One W.* Make your bed. *Another W.* Brush your teeth and do that 15-minute stretching routine you are not really in the mood to do but do anyway. *Two more Ws.* Choose some oatmeal and raisins instead of Frosted Flakes. Boom. Extend gratitude for waking up alive another day and visualize the best possible outcome for your next 12 hours. Now we're cookin'! These Ws compound to either diminish or improve our self-esteem and personal character. They radiate into the subconscious minds of others, subtly altering the way people relate to us in return. Setting yourself up for small wins is a moment-to-moment strategy for building character and should not be underestimated. Our favorite parts of the day should be when we catch ourselves in the mirror and upon seeing our reflection, realize we have become our ideal self, that we have something to offer the world, and that we can be depended on to fulfill our destiny.

Visualize yourself standing in front of a used car salesman with whom you are about to engage in some sort of interaction, maybe even a transaction. *Pause.* Now, imagine you are about to have the same type of interaction but with a Marine Colonel. Feel the difference? You expect one character to be shady (I realize I am stereotyping), and the other to be honest. The salesman might get a kick out of taking you for an extra grand, the colonel might save your life without thinking twice. The moment that precedes any interaction with another person, you will sense their cumulative displayed behavior. You have a front-row seat to the distilled essence of another human being's life experiences, for better or worse. But what an opportunity! You will sense their vibe. Now ask yourself, what do you want people to pick up from you? Because they will pick up something. That is certain.

Golf lets us choose wins (or losses) over and over and over again. I would rather lose a match and uphold the kind of integrity that lets me look in the mirror and appreciate what I see, than giving myself an unfair advantage while my opponent isn't paying attention. The veteran golfers among us know full well that the Golfing Gods always catch up with you, one way or another.

This game is self-correcting, which is part of its magic. When you least expect it, lipping out a two-footer is always right around the corner. Or how about a case of the yips? Dare I say the s-h-a-n-k word? The game of golf is an honorable one. A gentleman's and gentlelady's game. A game that expects its players to call penalties on themselves. Imagine carrying that principle out into your everyday life. "Hey boss, I know you were out, but I took an extra half hour for lunch." "Officer, the other day I ran a red light at 3:30 am when no one was around." "Honey, I threw a couple of my white socks in with a wash that was all colors." Funny, right? But on the golf course, that's just how it works . . . "Thanks, two-stroke penalty."

Simple, transferrable ways to uphold the integrity of golf on and off the green:

- Show up on time (or even a little early).
- Avoid being the slowest player in the group. Everyone loves to be in a rhythm.
- Don't be a distraction. Use courtesy and give others the space they deserve to complete a task their way.
- Care for the course. Fix ball marks and divots. Pick up after yourself and never litter. We are guests here on the green and on this planet.
- Don't lose your cool. Composure is key to remaining grounded and in tune with what the moment requires of you.

This subject is best summed up by the words of the legendary Ben Crenshaw. He said, "If we are to preserve the integrity of golf as left to us by our forefathers, it is up to us to carry on the true spirit of the game."

Golf has a spirit of its own, one that welcomes us to the first tee with open arms. The spirit of golf delivers opportunities to learn about ourselves, a safe space to examine what we are all about, and a sounding board that echoes back to us the areas in our lives that could use some attention. *Golf is a divine mirror of sorts.* Our sport should be honored as such. It deserves our humble and dignified conscientiousness.

I really wish we encouraged people in our daily lives the way we do on the golf course. It's just fantastic. Keeping our personal vibe positive and complimentary is a standard behavior worth modeling off the golf course. Extending and receiving appreciation are among the most valuable dividends awarded through playing golf. I never get tired of hearing "nice shot," and I never get tired of saying it either. It is common to witness PGA Tour Pros pause in the heat of battle to show appreciation for a competitor's good shot. Could you imagine a major league first baseman tipping their cap to a player on the other team after he hit a home run? Absolutely not. Never. But golf is so challenging that its devotees can't help but acknowledge a perfectly executed chip, putt, drive . . . anything really. This type of recognition is born of knowing everything that had to be taken into consideration to make that golf ball spin, bounce, stop, or curve. NOT acknowledging each other would be weird. Again, it's a gentleman's game. Sometimes I wish we lived in a gentleman's world.

An underestimated and underutilized human behavior is allowing others to encourage us. Sounds like a no-brainer, being open to receive, but it takes a great deal of self-love to absorb appreciation from another. We are taught to express humility, "Oh, I just got lucky" or "A blind squirrel eventually finds a nut" or any of the other countless self-deprecating cliches. And I get it.

Note to self: There is a big difference between humility and dismissiveness. I firmly believe opening ourselves up to receiving compliments is healthy, so why not let someone put a smile on your face for a moment? Early in my golf career, I learned from a sports psychologist that we must compliment ourselves equally and as frequently as negative self-talk. It is easy to allow negative self-talk during a round of golf since most of our shots will be missed. I'll say that again. *Most of our shots will be missed.* A 25 handicapper or a PGA Pro. Mostly misses. Because this game is hard. Period.

Upon asking my boss down at Boca Grove Country Club, Jack Schoenfeld, why he was not a tour pro, he wisely told me, "They have better misses than I do." If we're lucky, we'll hit a handful of dead solid shots per round. So, keeping this in mind, next time you receive kudos from a playing partner on a shot well-struck, let the love sink in because it is counteracting any accrued negativity. And for those solo rounds of golf, feel free to say out loud, "I hit that one great!" Sounds cheesy, but someone has to do the math.

Hole 5, Par 3: IMAGINATION

"Dream big and keep your dreams for yourself.
Because the dreams you have
are what separate you from others."
- Tiger Woods

While working at a private high-end golf club in the south of Florida, I often ran into sports celebrities like Paul Hornung and Rick Barry, to name a few. I preferred to hang with the shadier, craftier types. These players knew how to be gamesmen and made their opponents a little more emotional than they might've preferred. One member who fit that script was Wimbledon and US Open Tennis Champion, Bobby Riggs. Bobby let us call him "Riggs," which seemed perfect considering he was always trying to RIG something: asking for more strokes than he should've, claiming he was an 85-year-old man (he was 75), changing his bet mid-round ("*Didn't you hear me say double or nothing?*"), always needing a minute "to add up his score." You never wanted Riggs to give you his own score. Anyway, we played a lot of golf together.

Riggs was one hell of a storyteller, though I was warned by the elder club members to take his tales with a grain of salt. Still, I couldn't help but enable his proclivity for embellishment by tossing out softball questions to encourage follow-up, "So, Riggs, how much did you take that casino for? Wow! And the Presidential Suite too? No way!" My buddies and I would cackle about the yarn he spun. We loved his style, although most members couldn't stand his gamesman-type nature. Personally, I think they just took his showmanship too seriously.

Bobby savored getting under the skin of his stereotypically entitled country club member counterparts. Riggs' goal, he often reminded me, was getting you to beat yourself. His motto could've been, "I want you to know that I don't even have to beat you to win our match. I'm a natural winner and you are a natural loser."

I considered losing a match to Billy an honor. And that made him want to play with me even more. I loved observing which buttons of mine the wily old hustler would push in an attempt to get me to implode. In my mind, I was the one winning. I knew that an experienced competitor would try to beat me as efficiently as possible by attacking my greatest weakness. By letting Riggs' head games trigger me into an emotional state, I became more aware of my subconscious scars. This revelation opened me up to healing, which in turn helped me to develop mental toughness. (At least that's what I told myself.)

Riggs and I had a running match, a custom 9 holes, every Thursday at 4 pm. Riding around in his tricked-out private golf cart, he would dart out of his garage, which sat adjacent to the 10th fairway, to meet me at the 3rd hole. If Bobby was winning; he would just close me out and go home. If he was losing, however, he'd fake an injury on the 9th or 10th, click the garage door opener from his cart, and vanish faster than Wonder Woman in her jet. During those matches, Riggs taught me a valuable lesson about golf and life that I'd like to share. He taught me to never underestimate anyone at any time, including myself. Let me illustrate.

Bobby LOVED being short and right of the green. Why? Because it lured his opponents into making the unfortunate mistake of thinking they had him. Instilling in you a false sense of security was his ultimate weapon. If Riggs could turn your over-confidence into doubt, it'd be all but over except for your crying. I'd have a 12-footer for birdie and wind up three-putting for a bogey while I watched him get up and down for par from 20 yards away ALL. THE. TIME. Or if I had him down a couple of holes, he would "magically" hit the green in regulation. Combined with his handicap strokes, he could get the match back to square pronto.

I was born a year before the infamous Battle of the Sexes you see, and I knew nothing about tennis. That meant I didn't know Bobby had once been considered the best tennis player *on the planet*. I was oblivious to the fact that he'd won Wimbledon in 1939 *as an amateur*. Could you imagine an amateur winning . . . well . . . really ANY professional championship these days? I would love to believe that the money I lost to Bobby Riggs was not completely in vain but was a mere investment of sorts for you and me to learn from and cash in on.

This brings me to what I would now deem my greatest blind spot back then, *grave underestimation*. In the golfing sense, Riggs had the softest, most delicate hands you could've ever conceived. His ability to finesse a golf ball into landing exactly where he wanted it was like poetry in motion. Flyer lies, tight lies, rough, sand . . . it didn't matter. He could get up and down from the next hole's ball washer. Or worse, Bobby would just chip in. His game was crazymaking! Without any fanfare or fist pumps, he would idly walk up, take his ball out of the hole, walk to the next tee box, and watch you. I can still see him taking practice swings while yelling, "That's good!" a millisecond after my putt to halve the hole lipped out of the cup. Muscle memory, quick twitch reflexes, and spinning a golf ball were nothing to Bobby Riggs. But at the time, I was young and naïve. And all I knew was how to underestimate an old geezer. It was an expensive lesson, and I enjoyed every moment of it.

Eventually, not too long before passing away, Riggs taught me his biggest secret of all, that we wildly underestimate *ourselves*. One late afternoon, I let my discouragement and frustration show after having lost six of my last seven matches to Riggs. Seeing this, Bobby asked me, "Hey kid, do you ever picture yourself birdieing all nine holes in your match with me?" "Why bother?" I scoffed, "It's never going to happen." He said, "With that attitude, it can't happen. But theoretically, it is possible, isn't it? You know all the holes. Why is making a bunch of birdies so hard to imagine?" I didn't have an answer. And Riggs continued, "When I beat Cooke in '39 to win Wimbledon, I imagined winning every rally and every point. I primed the pump by getting my mind ready to win. Our subconscious doesn't know the difference between reality and imagination. It just takes what you give it at face value. Visualizing and feeling perfection PRIOR to good play will help when you experience the stress that comes with extraordinary success." "Why would success be stressful? I thought success was the point," I asked. "Extraordinary change in any form is stressful. Don't fool yourself by thinking that you'll know what to do when the time comes. You must prepare for it."

Soon after sharing his insights with me, Riggs' health began to decline. He passed away in October of 1995 in California. I wasn't able to attend the funeral but back at the club, we all toasted (and roasted) him for being the unique player and person that he was, golf aside. His slight stature induced well-trained, seasoned opponents to underestimate him, and he relished proving them wrong. I'm grateful to have known him and feel blessed to have received the wisdom I did from an old Pro, who defied physical odds over and over again throughout his life. In his honor, I do my best to never sell myself short and I hope you'll try to do the same. Just like Riggs, we can make par from anywhere so long as we believe we can.

Hole 6, Par 4: HUMILITY

I believe the greater the handicap,
the greater the triumph.
- John H. Johnson

NFL Head Coach Bill Parcells was infamously quoted, "You are what your record says you are." And he was right. This law is immutable. At the end of the day, your record is all you have. He was undoubtedly being hounded by a plethora of opinionated newspaper reporters with, "Your team should be this" or "Your team should be that." So out he blurts one of the most honest, obvious, straightforward comments in sports history.

Golf is no different. In fact, the handicap system is one of the greatest things about our sport. It allows for competitive matches among all calibers of players and gives us a reference point from which to track our improvement. It is, in other words, our litmus test.

Hitting pitching wedges at the range, 3 times a week for a month can bring your average score down pronto. I'd love to practice bombing my driver, but I know it's the wedges that get me closer to the hole more often than not and give me a chance to make par or better. I've learned that our Life Handicap (yes, I just made that up) also lowers when we are willing to move out of our comfort zone (driver) and into experiencing new situations (wedges).

We've got to be willing to do the tedious things in life, such as tidying our desk area, triple-checking our work for errors, or following up with customers who haven't yet responded. We must confirm meetings and appointments, complete household chores, and do a myriad of other tasks that keep momentum progressive. This tests our values while concurrently reinforcing who we are and what we believe in.

Lowering our handicap on and off the course takes time because permanent change requires integration. Two steps forward, one step back is actually a reasonable pace to shoot for. This is on account of the opportunities (or should I say lack thereof?) offered to us. It's not every day that a situation calls for a skill, talent, or behavior we've been actively working to cultivate. And when a challenge does arise, we tend to move out of the flow state by overreacting.

Parents will agree with me that it's not ALWAYS best to give children answers to their problems because failure (and the acceptance of temporary failure) is a great lesson in and of itself. Allowing kids to work through mental and emotional challenges builds character, resilience, and self-esteem. Subject matters change but the same principle holds true for adults. Patience creates a mindset that learns with time freedom instead of absolute urgency.

For lovers of life and golf alike, being patient with our skill development is key to enjoying the journey. Much like music, it's often the body of the work as a whole that enchants and inspires us, not just the huge crescendo at the end. Giving life (and our golf game) some time for an obstacle to manifest and ourselves some time to overcome the said obstacle requires patience. A wise player will use the time in between challenges to relax, breathe, and use positive affirmations to maintain a successful personal vibe. From this consciousness, strategies to surmount difficulty will arise effortlessly.

Golf is a humbling game, as we all know. One minute you think you've got things all dialed in, and the next you're secretly wishing you could walk to the parking lot and never turn back. Difficult times in life can similarly blindside us. A sudden passing . . . a lost job . . . a breakup . . . how we navigate these circumstances when they arise shows us the status of our Life Handicap. An open heart and mind allow us to glimpse the wider perspective offered to us from our inner guidance. And while this guidance may include concrete next steps to take, it is the momentary peace from receiving that intuitive support that ultimately stabilizes the difficult situation. Once grounded, we are able to choose the best option for the moment with confidence. Another technique is lowering the importance levels of day-to-day challenges. Having the presence of mind to honestly assess the urgency of a current conundrum brings much-needed mental space to the decision-making process.

In golf, we call making a crucial par after a double or triple bogey, "stopping the bleeding." It's not a birdie or eagle, it's just a ho-hum par to slow down and, hopefully, stop the current downtrend momentum. In life, "stopping the bleeding" could come from a simple act like giving someone a hug and letting them know they are heard. Most of the time though, it's best executed by *doing nothing at all,* by pausing instead of *reacting.*

We all know what it looks like in golf when things go from bad to worse. The pace of golf can leave us swept up in emotion, creating a mental grind, and demanding athletic execution. In life, however, there isn't always a 100-yard par 3 around the corner to settle things down. But mindfulness can lead your innate caddy to pull out just the right club at just the right time. *Trust your inner caddy to guide you.* It knows the course much better than you do.

To sum up the concept of lowering our handicap, here's an activity you may or may not like. Practice. I know what you are saying. "Practice? We're talking about practice. Not the 18 holes I just walked while carrying my bag. We're talking about practice." Yes. Practice. Practice makes perfect, right? Not necessarily. But perfect practice will make perfect.

And how can we know what constitutes perfection? Or perfect practice, as it were? By consulting our local golf pro or personal counselor. In doing so, we're admitting that there are aspects of our personality and/or swing we are unable to observe and correct alone. I may be a little passive-aggressive with my partner. I may be a little handsy with my chip shots. I may be losing focus at work. I may be lifting my head on my approach shots. Whatever it is, an experienced assistant can help.

Someone with the know-how to get us through a rough patch.

Time spent at the range repeating a new move can be likened to creating an affirmation. Muscle memory extends far beyond physical movement. We store emotional memory in the heart (which is coincidentally also a muscle). One excellent exercise is to engage in a verbal dialogue with yourself whilst imagining the feeling of realizing an ideal situation in your personal life. The practice is similar to visualizing your swing to prime the pump for a good golf shot.

In *Reality Transurfing Steps I-V,* Vadim Zeland says our highest intention for a situation can be set by our thoughts and feelings, and that we should visualize this "goal slide" in our mind. This image, or "goal slide" will become projected out onto our world, which will reflect back to us our ideal situation (our goal slide). In this regard, life is like a mirror. Instead of using our "inner intention" to force an issue and power our way to a new reality, we can use "outer intention" and trust the world to see and hear our desires and conspire to bring them into reality on our behalf.

You've heard the advice to "trust your swing." I couldn't agree more with the sentiment. But I propose we place our trust both in our swing *and* in our world to deliver an occasional kick-in birdie. After a series of bad holes, use your most comfortable clubs (no matter what they are) to find the fairway and green. Do this for the sole purpose of regaining confidence in your swing. Know that a solid easy bogey can be the eventual catalyst to solid easy pars. Giving up a stroke on one hole can pay dividends later in the round by recouping your swing. Mindsets like this one and those I mentioned earlier in the chapter bring your awareness back to the present, disrupt ineffective behavior patterns, and redirect reality to reveal your optimum experience.

Hole 7, Par 4: JOY

"Look deep into nature, and then you will
understand everything better."
- Albert Einstein

My mom, Barbara, loved golf. She was not a
habitual golfer by any stretch, but she loved the
game. The setting, the outfits, and the birdsong all
just did it for her. She was born in the '50's and grew
up in the Bronx. Her childhood was, in a word,
turbulent. On account of the domestic volatility, she
never liked being home as a kid. I imagine that later
on in her life, the quietness of golf brought her
much-needed balance. I'd see her among manicured
sand traps and smells of fresh-cut grass, watching
and smiling serenely as the little white ball soars
through the scenery. Her ball, yours, anybody's really,
just invoked joy within her.

You see, there's a stillness induced by our beloved
game that takes over when we watch someone's golf

ball fly. For us golfers, we're auto-calculating, assessing whether it needs to get up or down, whether it needs a hop, spin, release, and so on. Not Barbara. A decent shot staying airborne for a few moments was enough for her. Watching my mother appreciate the flight, in and of itself, was a wonderful sight. And it taught me a wonderful lesson.

The ongoing dialogue between humans and reality is the basis of our species' evolution. The conversation is displayed beautifully for the observers of a halfway decent golf shot. The transition between human activity (swinging) and our reality (the result) is on full display. Simply put, we act upon something, and then, the world takes over. During that moment of transition when we strike the ball, golf forms a relationship between us and reality. We are in total control of our swing until it is complete and then we are in control of absolutely nothing. There is a split second though, during which a third force comes into play, which is neither our effort nor our planet's gravitational pull. During this split-second mid-flight limbo of sorts, we release responsibility and accept our fate. Our game extends this magical moment to us as an opportunity to commune with the Spirit of Golf itself, and that communion is one reason golf is so positively addicting. The Golf Gods charm us via lucky bounces, good lies, creative spins, and fortunate breaks. We crave these mystical confirmations that work to assure us we are on the right track. Satiated only by making another tee time!

When I was a teen, my mother would take me to a Par 3 course called Rockland Lake Executive in Nyack, NY. She especially liked to go in the fall when the leaves were at their peak splendor and the air was cool and crisp. A pre-dawn breakfast at the Athena Greek Diner and off we'd head upstate, enjoying a foliage run on our way. These getaways were a happy time for both of us. So, what if she smoked with the windows up? It was chilly that time of day in October! Seat belts? Did they even exist in the '80's? She would sing Rod Stewart songs to me while I wiggled and danced like I'd seen videos of him doing on stage, broadcast from the newly aired MTV. About an hour's drive later, we would arrive; morning dew glistening along the first fairway, the mountain backdrop exploding with vibrant oranges, reds, and golds. Barely parked, people would hustle to get their shoes on so as to not miss a tee time. But we would move at our leisure. No rush whatsoever. We were in our own version of heaven. Why rush? We were already there. Peace. Serenity. Styrofoam cups filled with shitty coffee. You know, heaven.

Mom would chat with anyone. The pro, the cart guys, the Starter. Anyone and everyone. While I was on the practice green wondering about the course record, Barbara was sitting on the bench nearest the ball washer by the first tee. "Wow, that was a good one!" "You got all of that!" "Beautiful shot!" I'd overhear, not far off in the distance. Eventually, she would light up another Kool 100, call me over, and we'd pair up with another unwitting twosome. The sun's glare off the morning moisture was enough to scorch any retina, but nothing a little extreme squinting couldn't cure. Mom would play a hole here, a hole there, drop a ball wherever she wanted, and re-putt any time (which I really envied). She was so free, and she played by her own rules, bless her heart. She never kept score. She just enjoyed the experience. I, on the other hand, always leaned the opposite. Always trying to impress. Emulating Tour pros. Salvaging a par here and there. What can I say? I was a typical 13-year-old.

One beautiful morning, we came upon a hole that redefined my paradigm of playing a round of golf. It was a picturesque Par 3 from an elevated tee box. Nestled at the base of those gloriously colorful hills, we looked out onto a green that seemed a mile below us. Mom gazed down, soaking in every ounce of purity that morning had to offer. She never played this hole. She never needed to. This vision that my mother foresaw inspired her to arrange a golf date with me, her son, a few days prior. While I prepared for the hole-in-one of a lifetime, I looked over at my mom and recognized that she was in love. In love with the day, in love with her world, and in love with her son. Her own father, prone to flipping dinner tables, was forgiven. He'd introduced her to this game, which had led her to this moment now, and getting to watch her son's ball soar heavenward, pauses for that mystical moment, then rains down, down, down to the emerald circle.

A small trinket was buried at that hole upon Barbara's passing to ensure that her Spirit would forever rest with the Divine Par 3, and to link her new home among the clouds with that of her greatest experience of heaven on earth. Isn't this a wonderful game?

Hole 8, Par 4: MIRACLES

"Miracles happen every day.
Change your perception of what a miracle is,
and you'll see them around you."
- Jon Bon Jovi

As the social creatures we are, golf satisfies much of our innermost desire for connection. Generally, members of the human race prefer to share with each other what's going on in their lives, ask for advice, and just straight-up vent. Sometimes we do this over a bite to eat, hell, sometimes we do this over a cocktail or two. A much-needed distraction can go a long way in the wake of hardship, after losing a loved one, being displaced from a job, or living through a pandemic.

I played basketball with a bunch of guys twice a week until COVID-19 hit. Our gym was shut down along with everything else, so we banded together on the golf course to resume our comradery. We were fortunate enough to live in a state with a governor who kept the courses open so long as we were socially distanced. Xs were painted by the tee boxes 6 ft. apart, and a ball elevator was innovated, which let us use our putters to lift balls out of the holes. Necessity is the mother of invention, they say. On occasion, our group would play police officers to tri-state interlopers by enforcing the state protocols that ensured our hallowed local golfing privileges. We pulled through, along with the rest of the golfing world, and in the process strengthened our bond with one another. Weekly rivalries emerged for bragging rights along with countless stories about miracle par saves and the like.

Ever the optimists, our group once reassured a favorite teammate of ours who threw his driver into the woods in a fit of frustration, that he was currently the leader in the clubhouse at "one under in clubs." Sometimes, a teammate would be asked to step up and win a hole, or to donate some napkins to a partner who desperately needed to venture off into the woods after announcing, "it must be the tacos." These things happen. Our golf course is a judgment-free zone. (Not really . . . but you know, it sounded like the right thing to say.)

One of the golf course's Divine amenities is the

beverage cart lady. On a hot summer's day, you'd think those lovely lasses had angel wings, the way our group renders a "Hallelujah" that would be the envy of any local congregation. We created our own handicap system that states if any group is up more than two against their opponent, they have to chug a Fishers Island Lemonade. At 12% alcohol, the drink features a dynamic duo of Lemonade, Vodka, and Whiskey (Yeah, that's a thing). Having won my fair share of matches, I can tell you those bad boys get on top of you quickly. Sometimes a match can get away from you because of it, but on those hot, humid dog days of summer, I never mind.

Off the course, moments come out of nowhere that seem Divinely influenced. Simple things, like catching all green lights when you are running late and finding a perfect parking spot outside your destination. Things just line up. We give thanks in these moments as if we know somewhere deep down that something larger than ourselves is at work. In those situations, the outcome is perfect in spite of us, perfect even though we are not at our best. Maybe we feel we've cashed in some karmic chips or feel entitled to that kind of treatment from the universe.

What I can tell you is that the more we expect miracles to happen, the more they happen. Yes.

There. I had the audacity to say it out loud. The only catch (there is always a catch, right?) is that to receive a miracle, we must BECOME the miracle for someone else. We must open ourselves up to the universe to be used. The instructions do not emerge from our thinking minds. We must recruit our intuition. All we can do is prepare internally to act, provide, support, listen, assist, or display any other compassionate or helpful behavior for someone in need. We may know them. We may not know them. That is part of the mystery and also part of the fun.

Seeking out a mentor is one way to receive assistance with your current situation, on and off the golf course. Guides provide a labor of love by sharing their time, energy, and expertise with us and by imparting wisdom that undoubtedly took years to accrue. Those who mentor often feel they have received so much that giving back is the only way to make right on their abundance. Having a playing partner who provides real-time insights on course management or other strategies will save us years of time, strokes, and frustration. In business, mentors help us increase profits, provide encouragement when things stop moving at the pace we would like, and offer perspectives we may not otherwise see. I have been fortunate enough to have mentors who supported me when times were tough, and I look forward to giving back to others one day.

Sometimes we all feel depleted, left wondering whether things will ever get better. There is replenishment out there in the world, from good people who want to help, if we are willing to open the door. Humility is a powerful emotion, and people are drawn to those who reach out with it.

Fortunately for those of us here in Connecticut, we have a governor who knew full well that we golfers would need an outlet during the pandemic. I, for one, am grateful for the miracles in my life that used to go unnoticed. I strive to never forget the power of offering up a moment or two of my life in service to a higher power that works through me to bring miracles to others.

Hole 9, Par 4: WISDOM

"Golf is a game of misses, and the winners
are those with the best misses."
- Katy Whitworth

Accruing wisdom takes time, which is rarely on our side in today's fast-paced world. We feel pressured to push through challenges at all costs and achieve our end, justifying any force-feeding means along the way. I hear people saying, "There's just so much competition" and "If I don't keep pace, I'll fall behind." The heavy spell cast upon our society has created high standards for production, perfection, and value. While I appreciate the strive for excellence, high standards are a moving target. I sell electronics for a living and on account of the light-speed innovation of our time, many products are obsolete by the time manufacturers get around to training us dealers on them. Speed is a big deal right now, whether in the realm of food, manufacturing, or internet service. Thankfully the game of golf brings us back to a slower reality.

Try swinging too fast and you'll encounter problems. Walk the course too swiftly and you'll experience exhaustion. Try reading the green in haste and it's three-putt-city for you. Golf tunes us into a natural pace and gives us the time to take notice of wind speed/direction, putting surface nuances, and distances/club selection without rushing. This serves our long-term benefit by slowing us down enough to enjoy the round. It is my belief that increased enjoyment over time translates to lower scores.

The Ole' Pro is the fella you'll see sitting in a chair around the pro shop. Formerly, he may have been a scratch golfer but now he's the guy who just feels like hanging out. He might catch a little snooze now and then which is healthy at his age, but most of the time, he can be found imparting words of wisdom, which can only be acquired through years of golfing experience as an instructor. The slightest tweak from these sacred relics can enhance your game tremendously. I'm not talking about the old guy who thinks he knows everything; they are a dime a dozen. No, I'm referring to the geezer who says very little. A simple nod of the head can instill confidence powerful enough to save you two strokes a side. The disdainful raising of an eyebrow has forced more than one would-be golfer to quit the game and take up badminton. Without fanfare, he will recall striking a brassie out of the fescue to save par back in '43 or remind you of the time when the Bullseye putter was "new technology." He is the epitome of "been there, done that" and those wise enough to heed his guidance will forevermore be favored by the golfing gods.

Years ago, I had the good fortune of working at the Broadmoor Resort in Colorado Springs, Colorado, under the shadow of Cheyanne Mountain, home of NORAD. This setting boasted three courses, one of which hosted the 2011 Women's U.S. Open. Mountain golf at its finest. 300 days of sunshine per year and a ball that carries at least another 15 yards compared to sea level. Sounds like heaven, doesn't it? Broadmoor's resident Ole' Pro was none other than Mr. Dow Finsterwald Sr., winner of 11 PGA Tour titles, including the 1958 PGA Championship. From his deep well of experience, Dow shared his wisdom on the mindset and discipline required to take a golf game to the next level. I will always remember Mr. Finsterwald quipping "Are you sure you want to play that kind of shot?" I learned over time he was looking to hear back a resounding "YES!" He was able to recognize the moment doubt crept into my mind. Dow was testing my commitment to my chosen shot and helping me see that doubt creates weakness. In the game of golf, doubt is a BIG NO-NO. Win or lose, we must never second-guess ourselves. This Ole' Pro would instruct me to tell myself, "This is the perfect shot for me at this moment." Then, he told me to let go of all other options quickly and honor my commitment by staying down and through the ball.

So, it wasn't deep technical instruction that I took away from my brief apprenticeship with Mr. Finsterwald. Just a little something for "between the ears" that I use in my life to this day. Some solutions to our problems are tried and true, while others are more experimental. Whichever we choose, we must carry it out with 100% conviction.

My colleagues and I often debate about how best to design a security system for a home or office. While I understand that in theory there are multiple ways to secure a location from intrusion or fire, I must be committed to my design because, in my case, real lives are at stake. This motivates me to investigate deeply, conduct comprehensive research, and just straight-up work hard to find the perfect solution. I credit Mr. Finsterwald with a mindfulness lesson that has increased my confidence as a player and a professional.

Ultimately, the Ole' Pro is a spirit. It can inhabit anyone at any time. It's the voice of wisdom cutting to the quick and reminding us of the fundamentals we golfers are prone to forgetting. One of the most infamous ones is, "Don't be a hero and take your medicine." This humbling tip could have saved me from hundreds of strokes throughout my playing career. This advice is really so uncomplicated, but man oh man, do I love to complicate things. Like a kid, I don't want to take my medicine, even though I know it's the best thing for me. I want to be Tiger Woods and lay it all on the table. "No guts, no glory," I tell myself.

The quickest way to mess up a nine is with the dreaded triple bogey. This is especially frustrating when choking up a bit, punching out of the shit, and taking my medicine would have led to an easy bogey or possible par. We ought to listen wholeheartedly to the intuitive Ole Pro within us, sit back, relax, enjoy the game, and watch the results take us to the next level.

Hole 10, Par 3: NEGOTIATION

"In business as in life, you do not get what you
deserve, you get what you negotiate."
- Chester L. Karrass

Sometimes we have to negotiate with others, and
sometimes with ourselves. Either way, it can be tense.
In golf, our negotiating strategies can be very
revealing. How many strokes will you give up? What's
your match ultimately *for*? Will you go for that long
downhill putt? All is negotiated. And in each
negotiation, there is a wonderful lesson to learn in
how to barter and deal for the best possible
outcome. Especially when there are a few bucks on
the table. At the end of a round, someone usually
winds up forking over someone else's spoils of
victory.

Lee Trevino said it best, "Pressure is trying to make
a putt for a $10 bet with only $5 in your pocket."
Doesn't sound like a good negotiation if you are the

one putting, but a little "action" helps you focus and surprisingly, induces relaxation. If you feel any tension whatsoever, you are just about guaranteed to miss the putt, because nerves will take over and knock you out of rhythm. Done right, betting essentially forces you to be calm, centered, and relaxed. That's why guys like playing for money, I've learned. The best thing you can do is relax completely and trust your game.

In our life negotiations, we should be looking for a win-win solution. The win-win creates a mutual advantage wherein both parties can feel sincerely satisfied with the outcome. Many people do not know this, but the win-win scenario is integral in computer languages. Programs are written with computer code that contains an "If/then" scenario. "*If* the user enters this in the browser, *then* this website will load." It's automated, yes, but it is still a micro-negotiation.

In golf, the quintessential "If/then" is the standard "good-good." *If* I say your putt is good, *then* you say my putt is good." You see it all the time. Here's the key insight, though. The guy or gal suggesting the "good-good" doesn't want to have to make their putt. That's usually the deal. Early in the match (if you're up) it's ok, but rarely on the back nine. It takes the fun out of the game. Again, pressure relaxes us. Some folks would rather NOT know whether they can make the putt, which I myself cannot understand. You are out there to see what you're made of. Just give it 100%, trust in your stroke, and if you miss it, you miss it. There's always the next hole.

In life, negotiations are happening all around us, whether we recognize them or not. Ongoing compromises are what propel us forward. It could be settling on a price for a high-dollar item or opting for taking the back roads to avoid traffic. That little back and forth motivates us toward our goal. The key is to make up our minds, decide exactly what it is we would like to experience, and then allow the perfect negotiation to emerge before us. Without a clearly defined goal, fear of being taken advantage of or selling ourselves short will slow our progress.

FBI Negotiator Chris Voss tells us in his book, Never Split the Difference, that silence is a very powerful tool for getting the outcome we want. Silence gives the person we are negotiating with a chance to gather themselves and allow the last thing said sink in. It is also important for getting the other side to invest in the outcome. Ever hear the term "awkward silence?" That feeling is so unbearable to many that they will reveal information to dispel it.

Visualize for a moment that you are comfortable, confident, and relaxed during a perceived awkward silence. It could be during a date, while you're asking your boss for a raise, or haggling over the price of a new car. Feel for a moment how powerful that confidence would make you, and how much information you could gather via the subtleties of body language, the vibe of the atmosphere, and the intuitive thoughts emerging from your gut instinct. There is value to extract from those moments. As the proverb goes, "silence is golden." Use this tool's stillness to elevate your understanding of any situation.

The bottom line is this, there are countless things on the course and off the course that are better handled with a relaxed mind. Adding a little pressure to our game allows us to practice dealing with the pressure life can unexpectedly send our way.

Hole 11, Par 5: MAGIC

"Seeing ourselves win and wanting passionately to win
are the first steps to victory."
- Seve Ballesteros

In this chapter, we are going to explore the metaphysical essence of our game. If that feels a bit too far out for you at the moment, it's cool. No judgment here, and I'll catch you on the next chapter.

For those who choose to stick around, let's explore a few fundamentals of the golf game that you've probably had yet to consider, starting with the ball. Consider the golf ball an extension of you. A golf ball is round, just like our cells, just like our chakras, and just like our aura, which are all extensions of the self on an energetic level. The microcosm of the macrocosm, if you will. This connects us to the golf ball on a deeper level and thus, what happens to it causes us to emote. You may be saying, "but it's just a ball, right? It's just a game, isn't it?" I don't think so. Ask a professional basketball player how they feel about the basketball they dribble, or a soccer player how they feel about the soccer ball they kick around.

If you want to take your game to the next level, you must become the ball. Just like Tye said to Noonan in *Caddyshack*, "I'm gonna give you a little advice. There's a force in the universe that makes things happen. And all you have to do is get in touch with it. Stop thinking. Let things happen and be the ball. "We *are looking for that kind of magic.*

We invest so much in that little ball. Hours at the range, intense concentration, constant tinkering. We practice our shots until we feel it would be impossible for the ball *not* to land, spin, bounce, and roll, exactly the way we've intended for it to... effortlessly. *We do our thing and then the ball does its thing,* over and over again, until the expected result becomes forged into us. That's what it really takes. Oneness.

Are you a talker? I love talking to my ball. Not as much as, say, Jordan Spieth, but I do enjoy it. "Sit down ball!" "Bite!" or my favorite coined by Freddie Couples, "Boogie!" Why does it feel as if the ball might actually hear us? I offer the following theory. Perhaps, the relationship we have with the golf ball reflects the relationships we have with ourselves, and life in general. When we hit the ball too far and ask it to "sit," we are attempting to dis-create reality (choose a higher lofted club) and recreate reality (stop the ball) in real-time. We are basically asking the ball to defy the laws of physics. But hey, why not throw it out there? we think. You never know.

Take for instance, an imaginary golfer air mailing a shot over the green and telling it to "get down," only to find a ball dropping out of the sky and straight down on the putting surface. I'll tell you one thing, there is no way he or she is going to respond, "Oh, that wasn't fair. I'll just drop it in the bunker behind the green." As golfers, we are innately open and accepting of magic on the golf course. Pro, amateur, whomever.

But to see magic, you have got to put it out there. *You've got to be magic.*

I have fully embraced the philosophy that supernatural assistance is part of the golfing experience. So much so, that my opponents never fear losing a hole when I'm in the middle of the fairway, only when I've skulled, pull-hooked, or sliced my drive into the cabbage. I never get upset; I just accept that it's going to take some magic to pull off a par. And that my only chance in the world will require me to step back and let it unfold. If I TRY to do something, forget it. It was the *over-TRYING* that got me into the cabbage in the first place. I have to completely let go and let the magic happen. I've saved par more times than I deserve, and that's a fact. Maybe you have to. You'll never be able to accomplish alone what a supernatural force can. So, remove all the pressure and let that force take control.

Do y'all ever use positive affirmations? Still consider them too hokey? I tried a while back but eventually stopped because I felt too goofy. Saying words repetitively made me feel like a robot trying to program itself. Then I realized, affirmations aren't so much about repeating the same positive thing over and over again as they are about finding the feeling they are intended to elicit.

Let me explain: Kids learn multiplication tables through repetition. Over and over again, we repeat those number sequences until they become part of our subconscious minds, to be recalled when necessary. Recall learning those early math solutions. Through that process, we felt them become part of us. If the teacher scribbled 2 x 4 = 13 on the board, you could feel that something wasn't right, couldn't you? You didn't have to add the number 2, four times to prove the equation was wrong, you just felt it.

Repeating affirmations works because eventually, we can clearly, viscerally, imagine the feeling of our desired outcome completed. And that's where the magic begins to surface. When I'm in the cabbage, I imagine what it would feel like to tap in for par and walk off the green. That's my part. If destiny decides I shall make a par from jail, so be it. That's it's part. I do my best to let go of HOW I make par and focus on aligning with what par feels like. I could cut a 3 wood under the trees to the apron and get up and down *or* punch out and hit a 4 iron to 2 ft. *or* make a long putt *or* hole out from the sand. What do I care how it happens?

To realize any one of those outcomes, however, I have to find alignment with par first. A lot of golfers will say, "let me try to save bogey" and then get pissed when they lip out their par putt. All I'm asking is that you allow a little magic into your golf game.

Changing your life isn't much different. Simply asking for what you want can go a long way. I'm not kidding. It's all about asking questions. This is a hardcore life hack, so listen up. Our subconscious mind controls 90% of our lives. But our subconscious mind *is not rational.* Not at all. Not on any level. That means, your subconscious will believe everything you say to yourself, about yourself, about your life, your beliefs and then magnetize situations that reflect those beliefs into your life. Don't believe me? Think about the last time you had a nightmare and woke up in a cold sweat, heart pounding, SO glad to be awake. That's how real the subconscious assumes your thoughts and feelings to be; so real in fact, that you damn near felt like you were about to have a heart attack.

Thankfully, there is a method to curb the subconscious' madness. It takes repetition and finding rock-solid conviction. Unfortunately, you can't just pull a one-off, "I feel like I won the lottery!" and then head down to the quickie mart. It's a process, and it begins with asking the right questions.

As best you can, FEEL into what the following questions invoke:

- Why is my golf game so well rounded?
- How is it that I make all the right decisions during my round?
- Why is my swing tempo so perfect?
- How do I seem to have so much fun playing golf no matter the score?
- Why is making par so easy for me?

- How is it that my handicap gets lower and lower constantly?
- Why can I read the greens perfectly and effortlessly?
- How is it that I always trust my swing?

Now, imagine the golfer you are addressing with those questions is *you*. You can let your rational conscious mind beat the crap out of you later. But for a moment, pretend the golfer embodying all those desirable attributes is you. Take a deep relaxing breath and read the questions again.

Inhale.

Exhale.

That's the feeling. That feeling is what attracts the magical shot, par, round, or entire season for that matter! Remember what Bobby Riggs said, "In your mind, you can birdie every hole!"

You have to start somewhere by giving your subconscious something to work with. Repeat the questions outlined above on a daily basis and your subconscious mind will do the work of attracting the answers into your reality. Because that's what reality is: a mirror. Reality is reflecting your beliefs about yourself and your world. Beliefs that are projected from within you. So, hack your subconscious. Get in there and change your world for the better.

Pro tip: One thing reality is great at, is pretending NOT to be a mirror. Pretending NOT to be a 3-dimensional, holographic, image projector. Never forget that. On a daily basis, know within yourself that specific golfing or personal goals can and will be achieved. Then have the courage to get into a staring contest with your world. And DON'T BLINK! First off, you will find that reality means business when it comes to hiding its obligation of reflecting back our heart inspired and mentally focused desires. It will try to make you impatient and cave. Reality will say "you're wasting your time." And time WILL go by. It will explain "no, seriously, you're wasting your time." And MORE time will go by. These are reality's death-throes. You are inches away from the breakthrough you need to get closer to your goal. You just continue to take the INSPIRED ACTION that moves you in the direction of your desire. Act and feel with every fiber of your being that you are the golfer and person you affirm to be and do not wait for reality to catch up with you. By design, eventually, reality **must** catch up. Then enjoy the experience of observing your life calibrate itself around you. Without any fanfare take it all in, knowing that instead of steamrolling your way through life, you can allow a red carpet to be rolled out (to some extent). Reality doesn't know the difference in the way we get from Point A to Point B. It just creates the means that align with your goal without any judgment. Also understand that once the initial neural pathways are opened in your brain, the process becomes easier and faster. This is because our body/mind loves efficiency.

Now, develop your own questions that are specifically tailored to reflect your ideal game or life. Example Questions:

- Why do I feel so fulfilled all the time?
- Why do I have health and happiness in my life?
- How am I always in great shape?
- Why do people call me "Moneybags"?

You get the picture. Just have some fun! Resonate with the feeling, take inspired action when prompted, and allow reality to conspire on your behalf.

Hole 12, Par 4: IMPORTANCE

"To err is human, but when the eraser wears out
ahead of the pencil, you're overdoing it."
- Josh Jenkins

Fellas, you know when you tee your ball up nice and high ready to give it a ride, swing as hard as you can, and then flub your drive 11 yards in front of you, without reaching the ladies' tee? You become the living, breathing, personification of insult to injury. Because you are now obligated to drop your shorts and hit the next shot with your pants around your ankles. That second shot will be an initiation, should you accept, one of the more embarrassing lessons one must receive during their golfing career. Some guys will give you a pass, but others won't. It's a pride-squashing lose-lose situation. If you don't drop 'em, you're a chump. A lollipop, unwilling to honor the sanctity of the man code. If you expose yourself as expected, well, you're the dude swinging a three-wood in his bloomers. In the age of cell phone cameras, let's just hope you have playing partners who're more decent than mine.

My rite of passage came early, by way of my salty-sailor grandfather Artie, and two other Pall Mall-smoking World War II vets who hadn't cracked a smile in 30 years. There were a few things I did *not* have going for me back then after I hit my drive about 7 yards in front of the tee box. First off, I was 12 years old, and I wasn't wearing any underwear. Secondly, we were at Van Cortlandt Golf Course in the Bronx, not some private country club in the Hamptons, which meant that the idea of "proper golf course etiquette" was nonexistent. Thirdly, a group of ladies had just walked off the green adjacent to our tee box.

I remember nervously gesturing to Sully, my grandfather's Navy buddy and saying, "Do I really have to do this?" He told me I did. So, I asked him why and he said, "It builds character." I looked at Grandpa Artie with a tiny little tear starting to form in my eye and asked softly, "Is this what you did to build character too?" My sweetheart of a grandfather placed his strong hand on my shoulder and said, "No, grandson, I killed Nazis in World War II. You? You just have to drop your shorts, grab a 6 iron, and hit your ball into the goddam fairway before the chicks behind us try to play through."

The members of any brotherhood must adhere to a code of honor. So, I dropped my little pants, fixed my eyes on the ground, and sculled my second shot into the center of the fairway. After an embarrassing initiation, I was in. It was and will always be my favorite double bogey.

I knew my swing was the reason my tee shot didn't reach the ladies' tee. I had placed too much importance on swinging hard and hitting the ball far. Plain and simple. As with the game of life, golf teaches us that less is more. Trying too hard, no matter how well intentioned we are, will get us nowhere. Placing too much importance on outdriving your buddies and reaching a par 5 in two, is a recipe for disaster. Why? Because it knocks our swing out of balance. We must respect that imaginary meter, which vacillates between effort and ease.

On a macro scale, our universe is always seeking balance, so it should come as no surprise that seeking balance ourselves would benefit our golf game. Going overboard on anything triggers a corrective universal force, whose intention is to offset the excess. Reality Transurfing Teacher, Renee Garcia, illustrates this balancing force by asking us to imagine how different it would feel to stand on a plank that is 5 foot wide in our living room versus the same plank that connects two sides of a canyon. At home, you would feel relaxed when you look down. Not so much on the plank in the canyon. Balancing forces induce wobbly feelings. Walking that imaginary plank hundreds of feet in the air. If balancing forces could talk, they might say, "You are just standing there, what's the problem? You have excess fear? Might as well fall, already. The excess fear will vanish when you land! You'll be dead, but that's not my problem! The excess is my primary concern." Balance will always eventually be restored by the universe when things get wonky for better or worse.

The principle of Less Is More extends beyond the golf swing. For example, often in our relationships, we want to fix our loved one's problems when all they really need is to feel heard. Sometimes, being present is more than enough. Sure, we may have ideas that could help them move in the right direction, but at the end of the day it's their life to live, not ours. Our job is to support our friends and family in making decisions and show them the love they deserve to receive.

In our professional lives, excess importance can cause all kinds of problems. Collectively, we have been conditioned to place far too much of our focus on receiving accolades or making more money, than on increasing our value. A raise may provide physical, quantifiable evidence of one's self-value, but the validation it offers will be temporary at best. Generating value by conducting additional research, supporting other colleagues and just generally being an accountable team player will increase confidence and open up previously unavailable opportunities.

I encourage everyone to experiment with lowering importance levels. Allow yourself to lower the levels of importance you've assigned to a current situation.

Remember, this is just an experiment. Feel the emotional relaxation, the mental clarity, and the physical ease that comes with letting go of inner tension due to overfocusing. Take it down a notch or two. Pause for a moment. Tension blocks our ideas, visions, attitudes, solutions, and the like.

There are so many moments on a golf course where we say to ourselves, "This is a BIG shot" or "I've **got** to get this one close to the pin" or "I *have* to make this putt." I am NOT suggesting you try eliminating these thoughts and feelings. That would be impossible, and besides it's those moments that make our game exciting! What I AM saying is, just for a brief moment . . . pause and recognize the importance of your shot in relation to the world at large. This is not life or death. Tension will naturally drop, anxiety will diminish, your energy will be freed up to channel into executing the swing. Knowing self-induced stress was not a factor should render results that are acceptable regardless of the outcome.

Brooks Koepka, a former world's number-one golfer, informed us of what it's like to play this game better than anyone else. When describing the mindset of the current world's number one, Scottie Scheffler, Brooks said, "I know exactly what is going through his head. Nothing." If the best golfer on the planet can lower importance all the way to the top, we can use the same strategy to save a couple of strokes per round and watch our handicap shrink organically.

Hole 13, Par 5: HACKING

"No matter what calamities befall him
in everyday life, the true hacker still needs
the pressure and inconvenience of four hours
of trudging in wind, rain, sleet, or sun
(or all of them at once), hacking at a white pellet
that seems to have a mind of its own
and a lousy sense of direction."
- Tom O'Connor

I knew I was destined to be a hacker in the fourth grade. Not necessarily in the game of golf, but in the game of life. As a kid, I excelled in math. I was several grades ahead of my peers, competing in mathematics contests across New York City and tutoring my friends' older brothers and sisters on the side. It was an easy way to make a quick buck while my buddies and I were waiting for *MacGyver* to come on. Sometimes an older brother would throw me a couple pictures from his "girly mag" collection when he was too broke to pay me. Point is, I was really good at math.

Really, I think I was luckier than I was smart. One day in the fourth grade, our Japanese substitute teacher Mr. Ombe was walking around the classroom helping us individually with math. He drifted over to me and saw that I was struggling. Standing behind me, Mr. Ombe placed his two hands on my shoulders and slowly pulled me back in my chair to straighten my spine. He must have been some kind of Tai Chi master because immediately, both my mind and body relaxed. He whispered, "Puzzle." Then he said, "Puzzle come to you." And that was it. I'd love to tell you I was just smart back then, but the truth is that the smartest thing I ever did was listen to those words. He released me from the entire concept of mathematical "problems" by turning them into a game. *A game.* I never solved another math "problem" in my life, only puzzles. What really blew me away was realizing that the completed puzzle was already INSIDE ME. Allowing it to surface was the only real challenge. I would say to myself back then, "If I'm quiet and relaxed, then in time the way to win the puzzle game will come to me."

That's some next-level shit for a nine-year-old. And I just went with it. Mr. Ombe taught me that all the solutions are already out there, waiting for me to relax so they can emerge. The solutions WANT to come. I realized that figuring out the problem wasn't always necessary, and neither was dealing with all the anxiety, shame, nervousness, impatience, and everything else a kid goes through. The solutions actually want to come. That willingness to remain still and allow ideas to emerge feels like interfacing with evolution itself.

That day was a game changer.

Mr. Ombe helped me compete in all my NYC tournaments. He was an extraordinary individual who rightfully should have been addressed as Dr. Ombe on account of his PhDs (yes, plural) but was too humble. During our time working together, I found out that he had graduated in 1957 from one of the last grammar schools run by a Samurai in Hiroshima. That's right. An actual fucking Samurai. That meant if you acted up in class, you were sent to the office of a man who was armed with not only the stare of a laser but with a hammer-forged 400-year-old razor-sharp sword. Something tells me the paper airplanes in that classroom were all grounded. Anyway, another thing that struck me about Dr. Ombe was his shaved head. It bore countless deep crevices that looked quite bizarre to me as an adolescent.

119

Remember, this was back when the only fully bald people you saw were Kojak and cancer patients. His forehead extended back at a peculiar angle relative to his crown and the sides of his head tapered in towards his ears. I later found out that his disfiguring grooves were a birth defect, caused by the atomic detonation of Hiroshima. He had to keep his head shaved and clean to prevent bacterial infection. Dr. Ombe told me he felt lucky, that many of his peers' birth defects had been much, much worse.

Sometimes childlike inquisitiveness reveals parts of humanity we aren't quite ready to receive. The reality of his lived experience awakened me and opened my heart. I felt a deep connection to this human, who had accepted that for the remainder of his life having hair would be dangerous. My vain perspective on hairstyles back then dissolved and was replaced by sobering empathy for those just trying to survive this world.

Dr. Ombe never shared with me why his engineering career stalled. But it turned out that his awkward, yet harmless communication style was associated with Autism Spectrum Disorder. For him, dealing with professional and social interactions proved to be too challenging. I am truly thankful to have had the opportunity to learn from someone who overcame unfathomable obstacles and displayed admirable perseverance. To this day, the lessons Dr. Ombe learned in grade school and shared with me merged science and spirit, and have helped me piece together life's more puzzling challenges.

Here comes the hacking part. Nowadays, we imagine hackers as those tech wizards who break into computer systems by cracking the code to gain access to previously secure information. Usually, they do this for money, but sometimes it's just to mess with people. As a kid, I loved hacking mathematics because there were multiple ways to solve any single given math problem. Turns out, teachers just teach us the *formal* solution.

I couldn't understand why solving problems in a faster, easier, more fun way, was frowned upon. I just didn't get it. I saw the toll the "formal way" took on my younger sister Mary, who struggled in school. She was prone to migraines as a child that were beyond traumatizing to witness. I don't know if these two things were related, her difficulty in school and her migraines, but it's a possibility. Solving math puzzles differently was enjoyable, so that's what Mary and I did together during our tutoring sessions. As an older brother, I did whatever it took to make things easier for my younger sibling. Eventually however, I got called into our principal's office, where Sister Loretta was waiting to hand me my ass for undermining Mary's teacher. My poor sister had to deal with the teacher's frustration. I was no longer allowed to tutor anyone, which further confused me. I was disappointed because I loved it when other kids, a lot of them my friends, "got it." I enjoyed the look of accomplishment and triumph their faces displayed. It was a victory and there just aren't enough victories in the average kid's life.

"Life hacks" have recently blown up as an internet trend. On YouTube, you can find "how to hack" videos on just about anything. To me, hacking our human biology is one of the more interesting subjects. If you're ever bored, research Wim Hof aka "The Iceman" who cured the depression he experienced after his wife's passing, by allowing cold, something most of us work to avoid, to be his teacher. He was physically drawn to soaking in the coldest of waters, to being taught from the inside out, just how powerful we are. I speculate that in the beginning he felt drawn to submerging himself in cold water as a way of physically experiencing the pain he felt emotionally. In any case, he wound up learning so much about the body that he now holds multiple endurance-category world records. Wim

Hof works now as a teacher and motivation coach, whose optimism and joy have inspired millions of people to discover their internal supernatural powers and surpass the average human comfort zone. He hacked life in a way that revealed just how healthy, happy, and strong we are capable of becoming.

In the realm of reality creation, which for me constitutes the ultimate life hack, Neville Goddard, Vadim Zeland, and Stuart Lichtman, stand out as major players. Each work from their own modality, but teach the same lesson:

- Align your heart and mind with what you want to experience, knowing full well that in the vastness of the infinite realities, it *does* exist, and you will gravitate toward that experience.
- Let go of distractions, continue taking focused action, and allow the future to meet you halfway.
- Form a relationship with the infinite and know that the universe will conspire on your behalf to bring you exactly what you want, or something even better.

I love that we all start out as "hackers" on the golf course. Don't fool yourself, you were or are a hacker. In time, we convert our hacking into, well, hacking. We all overswing for a while and shoot 110 before eventually figuring out how to dial it back and advance the ball.

That's hack #1: Advance the ball. Easier said than done but hack #1, nevertheless.

Hack #2: Putt the ball near the hole, make or miss the next putt, then tap it in. These accomplishments allow you to play golf with anyone, anywhere, anytime, and that's a huge confidence-builder. In order to stop 3-putting, you must remove the 4-putt first.

Hack #3: Groove a swing. Find a rhythm. Mind you, you cannot take a million practice swings before each shot or putt, in fact the less thinking you do the better. Leave the thinking for the driving range. When you are out there, rhythm is more important than any thought you could have. Your body loves to be in rhythm and will reward you for respecting what it wants. Stay in the "zone" by staying in rhythm. You will see just how important this is when your 22-handicap playing partner simulates the PGA Tour on every shot and knocks you *out* of rhythm by making you wait. Every part of your body will say "this is NOT working right now." Find a comfortable breathing rhythm and keep your tempo steady.

There's nothing wrong with wanting to play better golf but try not to pay really close attention to your score. So long as your overall game continually improves, your scores will eventually reflect that. It is a nip-and-tuck strategy, and it takes time.

Hack #4: Fill out a scorecard for yourself with a whole bunch of birdies on each side. Give yourself some pars and a bogey or two to keep it real if you want. Make sure you put your name on it too. Whatever you need to make it as real as possible. Then, *feel* what it's like to shoot 95. Or 85. Or 75. Or 65. Keep the scorecard by your bed and look at it for a little while before you go to sleep the night before you are set to play a morning round. I don't want to say I dare you, but I dare you. Imagine as you are falling asleep that you are going around the course effortlessly hitting fairways and greens. See yourself getting up and down from the sand, draining long putts, short putts, whatever. Feel yourself laughing, having a great time with your pals. Notice a few dollars in your hand after the round, it can't hurt. Try it for a few rounds. You have to think of something while you are laying there before sleep anyway, don't you?

Hole 14, Par 4: ELEMENTS

"Weathermen merely forecast rain
to keep everyone else off the golf course"
- Larry David

We golf devotees like to think of ourselves as oracles, in tune with the elements, able to sense things before they happen. But then, we find ourselves on the golf course with a nice stiff wind blowing, "Hey there, it's me 'n you for the next 4 to 5 hours!"

Much like sailing, we must befriend the elements if we are to succeed. We can find reminders of this in sayings like, "When it's breezy, swing easy." The challenge to choose the right club and aim appropriately actually becomes enjoyable when we surrender to the weather and acquiesce to its influence on our golf shot. Hall of Famer Jack Nicholas often shares his experience of being on the practice green before a tournament round, listening to other golfers complain about the course conditions, forecast, pin placements, etc. They would go around airing grievances, and as each one took their turn, Jack would say to himself, "He's out. This one's done. That one I don't have to worry about." He knew that the initial outlook played a big role in determining the results of the game. After hearing Jack's story, I promised never again to psych myself out and that I would always just do my best and let the chips fall where they may. Weather and course conditions tend to be difficult enough without my adding invisible demands.

Striking a deal with Mother Nature requires us to take the highly recommended path of least resistance during a round of golf. Wind often vacillates between being an ally and an adversary. On some holes, we are helped by being downwind; on others, we are made to play right into the teeth of a stiff breeze. In Scotland and Ireland where the wind is rarely NOT blowing hard, golfers learn to accommodate with strategies like keeping the ball low and out of the wind, fading or drawing the ball into a crosswind, or taking two to three extra clubs on any given shot. We must commit to the shot in the same way the wind is determined to blow.

My home course is a public track called

Shennecossett in Groton, Connecticut. It's a Donald Ross designed links-style course on Long Island Sound, complete with wind, pot bunkers, fast domed greens, and fescue. It's a handful. And bless the owners' hearts, they keep it open all year. Playing through freezing temperatures in January is more of a male-bonding experience than a round of golf. Yes, whiskey is involved. We do what we must because resistance to poor course conditions makes getting through the round more like being punished than playing a sport. *Sometimes, we just have to let go and take what we are given.*

I consider strong winds a great teacher. It'll teach a player how to "knock the ball down" by keeping it low and out of the wind. The knockdown shot is also my favorite shot in the world. Why? Because it is humbling.

If you intend to have a good experience in golf or in life, humility is a requirement. I often hear a little voice in my head say, "Humble yourself or be humbled." I wish I could tell you that growing up I heeded my own warning, but it would be a lie. Generally speaking, life gets much easier when you humble yourself before life steps in to do the job. Sometimes, that requires pulling out a 4-iron or hybrid off the tee just to find the fairway. Humility will ask you to swing easy, remain disciplined, keep your backswing and follow-through low, play short of the green, and let it bounce up onto the green like our ancestors in Scotland did. I love this golf shot because even when the wind is calm and you don't need to knock it down, you can still use it on a day when your normal swing is not cooperating. It's my default emergency swing and has saved me during a lot of rounds. The knockdown shot is like an old friend that says, "I know your game is a little pear-shaped right now but relax, we'll keep this respectable." A well-executed knockdown shot rarely gets you in trouble, much like a humble life.

Hole 15, Par 4: CONFIDENCE

"Always make a total effort,
even when the odds are against you."
- Arnold Palmer

My favorite club is my 1 iron. Yes, you read that right. If you are newer to golf, you may not know what the hell I'm talking about, but Hall of Fame golfer Lee Trevino once famously said, "You could stick it in the air during a thunderstorm because even God can't hit a 1 iron." For an iron, it could not have any LESS loft. The face of the club is SO upright that you could mistake it for a putter. Seriously.

I never liked the rap the 1 iron gets. It's an iron, plain and simple, and I hit it like I hit my irons. Someone needed to make the 1 iron their friend and that someone is me. I feel happy just pulling it out of the bag. And outdriving my buddies with it (on occasion) makes me feel all warm inside. People don't know that I've hit thousands and thousands of

1 irons on the range. The reason? You guessed it. I can't hit a driver worth shit, and somewhere along the line, I got tired of looking for my ball. It's not so complicated, is it? Someone could suggest I hit a 3 wood which I often do, but I can hit the 1 iron just as far, so why not? It has a mystique to it, and I wanted it to become part of the lore. It intimidates other players to a certain extent and being a small guy, all of 5 foot 7 inches of me, I rarely incite a feeling of fear in my opponents.

Any iron off the tee is a "fairway finder" and sometimes, on some holes, you just HAVE to get it in the fairway to have any chance at par. It's a club that can only go so far, right? It's an iron. You can't hit a 6-iron 265 yards. But the driver? Who knows how far the ball will go? Guys like me score better when we take the Superman variable out of the equation and settle for 230 down the middle of the fairway. Plus, it makes me feel confident in my long iron game, because, well, it has to. After hitting a 1 iron off the tee, you have a lot more 4 irons into greens than 8 irons. The secret that I learned was that confidence with long irons translates exponentially to short irons. After hitting as many long irons as I've had to, I salivate at the feeling of having a 7, 8, or 9 iron in my hand. I have a good chance at birdie every time.

No question about par. That's a given. It's all about birdies now.

I share this with you because golf and life are all about mindset. Learning to defy the odds and master something others might find difficult or damn near impossible will impact your overall confidence. For some, it may be chipping with a 7 iron, for others it may be hitting a super high flop shot that stops right where it landed. In life, this principle may translate to learning enough Chinese to order food at your favorite local restaurant. Maybe for you, this looks like learning to drive a stick shift, or play one song on the guitar, or cook your favorite dish. Find something you can do that makes you feel like, "I got this." I am here to remind you that newly mastered abilities create a ripple effect in your life that will encourage you to accept newer, greater challenges you would not have even considered undertaking a year ago. You will experience a newfound respect and appreciation for yourself. Going forward, remove any need to think inside the box. Exercising our freedom to think outside the box leads to interesting skills, newfound creativity, and lower scores. Mark my word.

Here's another fun example: Every now and then, when you are around the green, have your playing partner pull the flag regardless of where the ball is. If you are any bit old school like me, I assume that when you are putting, you like to have the flag out. If not, well, you can skip this part. When you pull the flag, you are setting an intention whether you know it or not. You are saying, "I plan on making this." That is your intention: Success. When we are chipping, our thoughts tend toward, "Let me hit a good chip, and hopefully it's close enough that maybe I could make par. I missed the green, so I guess a bogey isn't too bad and blah blah blah." You can think that any time you want, but every now and then, please, for the love of Bobby Jones, try saying to yourself, "I'm going to make this one." Have the guy or gal who is marking their ball up on the green pull the flag. Have them pull the flag just like when you are cleaning up a two-footer for par and they are standing next to the hole. They are taking the flag out because you plan on making this one. And that is a great mindset. Say to yourself, "I am going to defy the odds. I'm going to make it." Some will say you have better odds of making it because the flag can help you by being a backstop of sorts. But your chip would need to hit the flag perfectly square for that to be true. Also, a PGA Tour statistic showed that only 11% of balls that hit the flag actually went in. Anyway, what I'm trying to tell you is that the right mindset will lead you to hitting the right shot that drops right in the hole whether the flag is there or not. This exercise is about mindset and confidence. Give it a try, you know, for fun.

Hole-in-one. Ever gotten one? Talk about defying the odds. I'll be honest, I've never gotten close. Yeah, I've hit it to a few feet, maybe even closer, but never stood on the tee box and said, "That could go in!" Not yet anyway. A buddy of mine who has played more rounds than anyone I know, has never had one. But my cousin's wife? She has seven. My dad has three. It is an elusive phenomenon that defies all odds.

Maybe you have carded an ace yourself or been there when a partner did. It's a wonderful part of the game, a day to always be remembered even if you just happened to be at the bar in the clubhouse. (Hey, traditions are traditions.) I write about the hole-in-one because what other game allows you to dream 4 times per round? Every time you step up on a par 3, you have a chance. How exciting! What a game. This game allows you to fantasize like that. Imagine someone playing in an official basketball game and just heaving the ball to try to make a full court shot! And then his teammates come over and say, "What are you doing? There's, like, 4 minutes left in the 2nd quarter!"

Hole-in-one in life? Ready ... and ... go. Sending out that resume for your ultimate job and landing it, playing a lottery game and coming up a winner, asking your crush out on a date and getting a yes, landing a gig opening for your favorite band, scoring tickets for the big game or sold-out show, closing the big deal, having your offer accepted on your dream house, finding out you are going to start a family, acing your final exam, the list goes on and on. These experiences are what make life worth living. Every now and then, life asks you to dream big and then accept that dream when it becomes reality. Our job is to feel like we are living our dream before it becomes a fact. The trillions of mini miracles that happen just within our bodies on a daily basis warrant awe.

When we reach out with a vision for a better day, a better shot, who knows? It may just find the back of the cup.

Hole 16, Par 4: HAZARDS

"To me, from a competitive standpoint,
golf is the hardest game to play."
- Michael Jordan

We encounter obstacles throughout our lives, both on and off the golf course. Some we glimpse on the horizon, while others emerge rather unexpectedly. Upon encountering one of these snags, complaining to anyone willing to listen is an easy default. But whether we air our grievances or keep quiet, they ultimately need to be dealt with. Carefully. Some very carefully. Our challenges only continue to grow when we refuse to ask ourselves important questions such as: what are my options now? What am I capable of? What are my strengths and weaknesses? These are questions all of us would do well to answer honestly.

Thinking about such things calls to mind Dustin Johnson. DJ was playing in the PGA Championship at

Whistling Straits, oblivious to the local ground rule regarding waste areas, which were distributed to all the caddies prior to starting the round. DJ grounded his club in a hazard, and this resulted in a 2-shot penalty
along with the ending of his bid at a major. Golf teaches us that committing the tiniest of miscues at the wrong time and place can bring about harsh and seemingly unfair consequences.

Not being able to ground your club in a hazard is just one of many challenging golf rules. We deposit our ball in the bunker and are then forced to get ourselves out with zero improvements to our lie. *We must negotiate with the sand to save the hole.* In some cases, negotiating with life may also require a delicate hand. Ever been in a situation that demands your ideal word or deed? The kind of situation where you are acutely aware that anything less will make things worse? Sometimes, going backward will be the only play that makes sense. We saw this on the Pro Tour in those British Open pot bunkers. Just like in life itself, when a heated argument escalates in volume, a deep breath and an honest assessment proves to be invaluable.

Any dream interpreter worth their salt will tell you that water symbolizes emotion, regardless of whether it takes the form of an ocean wave, lake, or squirt gun. These soothsayers must be right because when I encounter water during a round of golf, it's usually yelling for me to "GET UP!" with a lot of . . . um . . . emotion. Taking the water out of play is paramount to keeping our scores low, which I do realize is easier said than done. Start by replacing the water with an open fairway in your imagination. Feel the emotional charge associated with the water. Feel it dissolve into a fairway. Visualize your shot executed perfectly and take a relaxing breath. This won't guarantee your shot stays out of the drink, but it will ensure the hazard *threat* doesn't affect your shot.

In life, allowing ourselves to become swamped by the nautical fluidity of emotion can prove both destructive and expensive. Wars have been fought; fortunes lost. Why else would we say that conflicts reach a "boiling point"? Spending too much time in an emotional whirlpool can cause us to make hasty decisions, which are not always in our best long-term interests. Hurrying just temporarily ends the suffering. And I get it, because, in moments of stress, I just want the discomfort to stop. So instead of dealing with the discomfort, we bargain, telling ourselves if the decision turns out poorly, we'll figure it out later. It's the *avoidance* of our emotion that aggravates our initial predicaments.

Bringing awareness and breath to our emotions moves us through them, or them through us as it were, and more quickly alleviates the discomfort. How? Practice breathing in 'acceptance' through your nose, right down into your diaphragm, and then breathing out 'stress,' all the way from your belly. After a little while, remain still and allow your consciousness to present you with its objective and judgment-free solutions. Try on each new feeling, each new solution, and see which one resonates. Believe it or not, this is what transpires when we are, say, in-between clubs. Big 9 or Baby 8?

I don't know about you, but I get a little pissed when I hit a great drive down the middle and don't know exactly which club to then use on the green. A similar feeling crops up when I'm at work and want to run a proposal by my boss. My brain starts up, "Should I have 200% confidence and speak boldly or put the kid gloves on and tiptoe through the pitch?" There are no gap wedges at my office, unfortunately, and little time to breathe and let the perfect solution reveal itself.

Talk about hazards, how about OB? Oscar Bravo. White stakes that surely emerge from the pits of hell. Do we even have to discuss this? When you hit it out of bounds, you're fucked. No other way to say it; penalized severely and mandated to start all over. Humiliating. Humbling. Horrific. Just one ball OB can ruin countless front 9s and back 9s. And all with just one swing. Because that's all it takes, one swing. I have a regular playing buddy who, if I were to hit 6 inches OB, would make me walk back to the tee box and re-tee. Bless his little German heart. He doesn't care who is on the tee behind us. "Rules are rules," he says. "Hit a provisional next time," he tells me.

I learned the best way to avoid OB from LPGA Pro, Michelle Low. She prefers not to concern herself with where the white stakes are. She says, "Just pick a target far in the distance that lines up with your shot and try to hit it." The trick is in making the target small, like a leaf or a branch far off in the distance, much further than you could ever hope to hit, but that is on your line, nonetheless. This brings hyper-focus to the direction you want the ball to go, rather than to whatever it is you're trying to avoid.

Winding up out of bounds in life presents another intense challenge altogether. I'd rather hit it OB on every hole, than once in the game of life. You can die. You can take someone else's life. I know, shit just got real, didn't it? But think about it for a moment. Veering off course in life creates a tangent in your lifestream, which often cannot be undone. Having one too many drinks and getting behind the wheel of a car, for example, has no doubt led to countless irreversible tragedies. And like in golf, one has to live with it. You make amends, correct your behavior, stay committed, and learn from the experience even, but you never forget. There are good people out there, who went OB just once and are now incarcerated. Good people who made one bad decision and now live without basic freedoms. Stories about these types of tragedies make past arguments with partners and friends, and the subsequent apologies, seem like a walk in the park.

Hazards are part of the game and part of life. I believe they exist to challenge us and direct us toward doing the right thing. Ever seen a pro golfer in a pot bunker during the British Open? Often, the best golfers in the world choose to come out sideways, or even worse – backward. This avoids making a bad situation worse. No matter the obstacle, find the advantage hidden within.

Hole 17, Par 3: LESSONS

"I never played a round when I didn't learn
something new about the game."
- Ben Hogan

Sports are special because they offer a constant avenue for learning. Let's take the first interface you have with the game of golf and observe what happens for a moment. There's the club and there's you: two separate things. You reach out and grab the club by the business end, sliding the shaft down your hand unconsciously until the club head is on the ground and you feel something rubber in your hand. Then a second hand enters to join the sport. The club is now gripped, perfectly, permanently. And two things become one. Club in hand, we are ready to accomplish something extraordinary. By joining your two hands together with that one club, you gain the power to move a small round object no less than 800 ft. away from you in roughly ten seconds. If that isn't special, I don't know what is.

The first lesson is always the grip. That's where it all begins. "It's like holding a baby bird," they tell you. "You don't want to kill it and you don't want it to fly away." Pinky and index fingers on the back side of the club interlock, overlap, or rest side by side. The thumb and index fingers form a V which points to the opposite shoulder. This is called the neutral grip, and I was told by my grandfather to never, ever, ever, change it. "What happens if I do?" I asked him once. He grabbed my collar and said, "Incarceration. Do what I say, and you'll stay out of jail." I thought that was kind of dramatic, so I laughed it off. It wasn't until years later that I realized what he meant.

You see, if you have a neutral grip but a bad swing, changing your grip can produce a little bit better result. *A little bit.* But it's still lazy. "Wow, my ball doesn't slice as much," or "My hook is now a draw," you will tell yourself. But now you are imprisoned by that ball flight. You have locked yourself in with no way out. The object is to hit the ball straight, moving it left or right only if the situation calls for it. *You control your ball flight*, not the other way around. Thus, fixing up your swing by working with a local pro is the answer.

Let me offer an analogy or two. Ever seen

kindergarteners walking in or out of school together? It's one of the sweetest visions in the world because they always hold hands and walk in a line. The teacher simultaneously promotes unity, order, and togetherness, while making it easier to get a head court on a bunch of five-year-olds. Gender and race have not yet skewed their little minds toward judgment; their grip on reality is largely still neutral at that age. They are only just learning about life. But if they experience something traumatic during those impressionable years, it is possible they will begin to associate negativity with gender or race. Without correction via compassion and forgiveness, stereotyping is born. Their perception of others can become altered, which may then get reinforced by their parent's behavior and language. You can see we've got a mess on our hands now and the situation must be neutralized. If the balance is not restored ASAP, there will be issues going forward.

Or imagine yourself in the middle of a herd of ten horses. You hold up a shotgun and fire. The horses scatter, right? Those big ears do seem particularly sensitive, so that's fair. But when horses are introduced to harsh and impulsive sounds as mere foals, they become desensitized. At first, trainers will discharge fire far away so as to not hurt the horses ears but as they grow older, they move closer and closer. By the time they are grown, a rider can sit still in their saddle and fire a gun repeatedly without the horse moving a muscle. Just check out the Single Action Shooting Society, which travels America showing off our cowboy heritage.

These illustrations simply show the importance of maintaining neutrality. Adjustments can be made from this balanced place toward creating permanent, positive change. *No quick fixes.* Tinkering with your grip is like duct-taping a leaky hose in your engine. Eventually, the hose will need to be replaced. So, if your ball flight is a little too wonky to get you around the course with ease, refrain from tweaking your neutral grip, pony up the money, and call your local pro.

Hole 18, Par 5: BELONGING

"Love and belonging are irreducible needs
of women, men, and children. We are biologically,
cognitively, physically, and spiritually wired to love,
to be loved, and to belong."
- Brene Brown

Make no mistake, we are social beings. The more logs you burn in a fire, the more energy you will create. I recently sold a CCTV camera system to a renewable energy corporation in Connecticut. The reason was, if someone were to fall asleep on the job and forget to add wood to the industrial burners, the power could go out. Not only in the town where the company is located, but in all the surrounding towns, too. Talk about the importance of energy creation!

Participating in a golfing club is a fun and worthwhile experience for players at any level. Meeting others with the same passion for the game creates a little spark because it gives us the opportunity to hear new stories, learn new skills, and laugh at new jokes. Playing a round of golf with new people can reveal a lot about how we show up in relationships with others. The course exposes our strengths and weaknesses.

If you were to consider the handicaps along with intangible strengths and weaknesses of each player, pairing up golfers for a large outing would require a mathematician. But even without Dr. Ombe, somebody steps up to uphold the spirit of fairness and the teams will be set. There will always be a few outliers who keep to themselves, but for the most part, I experience an overwhelming sense of unity anytime I get together with a gaggle of hackers. I've always appreciated that, and I hope you will too. Even the fella pounding beers and shooting 117 would probably tell you he'd do it all over again. *After all, it's just a game*, and as challenging as the game can be sometimes, we are just out there to have some fun.

Then there is the piece about getting to experience strength in numbers. We have all been at the 19th hole, relaxing after a round with the lads and lasses, and felt the rumble of what can only be called a herd of golfers entering the clubhouse after waiting for everyone in their group to finish. The laughter, finger-pointing, stories, and occasional taunting brings the volume of any establishment up to 11. You've got The Accountant who makes sure that no one forgets Barney's strokes on 4 and 13 and reminds everyone that there's a hot wing special and 2-for-1 Bud Light on draft. Then you have The Comedian who loudly recounts Virgil's whiff in the rough on 17 that was the deciding factor for his team's 1-down loss. The Taxman visits each table collecting score cards and double-checking for John Hancocks. The President has both his hands up, encouraging the constituents to keep it to a dull roar out of respect for the locals at the bar. The Salesman is trying (in vain) to work out a deal with the head pro for the next outing, consisting of 15% off greens fees and a complimentary bag of tees for each group. The Show-off makes rocket gestures with his hands while describing the trajectory of the self-proclaimed 300-yard bomb that he hit on number 14 despite shooting 112. And finally, you have The Underboss divvying out any funds that went into the prize pool. Where's the Boss you ask? He's with the Salesman making the pro an offer he can't refuse.

Here are some general benefits to connecting with a golf group, or any other community for that matter:

- **Motivation**. When surrounded by people making moves, it can inspire and motivate you to do the same.
- **Learning Opportunities.** Everyone knows a little something you don't. You can reach out to your community to ask questions and get advice.
- **Make Friends.** Making friends can be difficult, especially as you get older. Being part of a community gives you the opportunity to meet and bond with like-minded people.
- **Networking Opportunities.** Whether you're in need of a service or you have a service to offer, it's likely your peers will have introductions for you.
- **Stress relief.** Community events give you the chance to interact and have fun with others, which in turn, can relieve stress. Humans are social creatures by nature.

According to a study published by BMC Psychology, which included 9,119 men and women from England, Scotland and Wales, social engagement through civic group activities is associated with better cognitive function at age 50.

To investigate associations between people's social engagement throughout their adult life and cognitive function at age 50, the researchers used data from the British National Child Development Study (NCDS) and a general population sample in England, Scotland, and Wales. Baseline data was collected at birth in 1958 and study participants were followed up at several points later in life. At age 33, 83% of all respondents reported that they did not participate in any civic organization. By age 50, the number drops to 64. As we age, *relationships* become more important in experiencing an enriched life. Our instinctive understanding of "strength in numbers" plays itself out.

Out of the overall sample, 8,129 participants completed cognitive tests at ages 11 (reading, writing, math, and general ability tests) and 50 (memory and visual attention, speed, and concentration tests). The researchers found that almost a third of the sample population's cognitive ability deteriorated between ages eleven and 50 when community activities were put on the back burner. A quarter of the participants showed improved smarts at age 50 by scoring higher in cognitive tests (except that one dude who cheated). Also, participation in each *additional* civic group was found to further increase test scores much like a parlay with your local bookie. This study shows scientifically that we're smarter and stronger together.

And not only that, but the more groups that we join, the more our overall capacity to problem-solve increases, as well as the ability to support a mutual goal and develop new skills. I recently experienced this when I met with a customer of mine who, at the age of 92 (without tech support or intervention from the grandkids), learned to sync his new iPhone and iPad, and his wife's Android and tablet, directly to their printer. He told me about the two committees that he belongs to at church. He prints their agendas. His participation in his church community motivated him to find a YouTube tutorial and give it a try. *Where there's a will, there's a way.*

Everyone can find a place within a group and garner a sense of belonging. Belonging is one of the most incredible feelings that we get to experience in this life, and regardless of who you are or what you are doing, you deserve to bask in it. Welcoming others into a group and being welcomed are two sides of a very primal coin. Human beings have delicate feelings and sometimes it feels like this world actively seeks to undermine our sense of belonging. It is our obligation as humans to remind one another that we *all* belong here. *If we didn't, we would be somewhere else.* But here we are, and we are in this thing together. We could be 3 down with 4 to go, we could be pitching our product to venture capitalists, we could be on the front lines fighting the good fight, or we could be supporting someone in need. Whatever our outcome, whether we win or lose, we are all in this together. Until the end. And that's that.

In the Clubhouse

My theory regarding life is that it emulates an individual's golf game. This book is a literal reflection of that theory. There is no escaping golf-life integration for me at this point. The front side started off solid. I hit it stiff on the amusing Par 3 5th hole and tapped in for birdie. I kept the pace with Joy in the Par 4 7th with an emotional recollection regarding my late mother's ability to bond with me over our beloved game. Good tempo and a nice rhythm. The pace of the play was comfortable.

However, things started to go pear-shaped when I made the turn. The Par 3 10th on Negotiation could have been more comprehensive. I tried to make up for it by reaching the subconscious-oriented Par 5 11th in two but ended up with a fried egg in the greenside bunker. I hacked my way to a bogey there. Ironically, the Hacker story on the Par 4 13th is what got me back on track and saved the round. Holes 17 and 18 were solid even though I was a little tired. But I kept my breathing in check and squeaked out a few more pars. All in all, a good round or in this case, an easy read.

Clearly room for improvement, but I will sign my scorecard with pride this time around. Truth be told, I realized three-quarters of the way through, that I wrote this book for myself. Each chapter-hole is a reminder of how I want to live my life, on and off the golf course: with humility and gratitude, with calm focus, with a curious mind and an open heart. My experience is enriched, no matter the circumstances, when I am living in alignment with these principles. It's easy to forget ourselves and lose our bearing, what with the pace of life and all. Circling back to the ideas that keep me grounded and relaxed is a must, since things can go pear-shaped pretty quickly nowadays.

I never wanted to be an author. I do not like writing. I can barely type. This whole book was written with 2 between 2 am and 5:30 am, go figure. But I went to bed early and embraced being fully rested and totally inspired at an hour some would call God-forsaken. In doing so, my sense of self changed in a profound way. I realized that when I have a passionate vision, but not enough hours in the day to bring it to fruition, life will somehow squeeze out 3.5 energized hours to make that desire a reality.

Now that I've put a bow on this bad boy, I am ready to get back to some nocturnal normalcy. I'm sure my wife is too. The point is that sometimes we have to step out of our comfort zone to grow in a way we could not have anticipated.

As you can imagine, some of these chapters were very cathartic and, ultimately, I feel that writing them has supported my healing as a human being. Others were just fun, like the one about the history of golf. I really enjoyed googling the sport's actual origins and then straight up spinning a yarn on how I imagined it all going down. I hope you got a chuckle as well. I hope you gleaned a thing or two that will save you the strokes you rightfully deserve.

I'll leave you with this:

Breathe. Relax. Give. Appreciate. Learn. Trust. Encourage. Love. Golf.

THANK YOU!

Heartfelt appreciation and love to my wife, Kimberly, for your encouragement, support, and expertise. This project was graced with your keen eye and experienced touch, and I am forever blessed to have you in my life.

I'd like to thank my course cronies for their relentless enthusiasm and heartfelt passion for the game that we love. Rando, Ace, Train, Jay, BC, Marcus, Skip, Joey Q, Arthur, Roger, Carl, Rick, Murph, Lance, and all the punters who play over at Shenny on the regular. Shout out to my main man Palazz, for his ability to peer pressure all of us and turn Tuesday afternoons into something special.

Big love to Gerald and Beth Todd for sharing their faith in the Holy Spirit and their love for a game that is clearly Divinely dispensed.

Special thanks to Don M for taking me golfing on my birthday and his patience while I got pulled over by the cops. That's a story for another day.

Made in the USA
Middletown, DE
01 November 2025

19598227R00089